MATHEMATICIANS

MATHEMATICIANS

AN OUTER VIEW OF THE INNER WORLD

PORTRAITS BY MARIANA COOK

American Mathematical Society

This book was first published in 2009 by Princeton University Press, 41 William Street, Princeton, New Jersey 08540. In the United Kingdom: Princeton University Press, 6 Oxford Street, Woodstock, Oxfordshire, OX20 1TW

2010 Mathematics Subject Classification: Primary 01A65

For additional information and updates on this book, visit www.ams.org/bookpages/MBK-116

Library of Congress
Cataloging-in-Publication Data

Names: Cook, Mariana Ruth, author.
Title: Mathematicians: an outer view of the inner world / portraits by Mariana Cook.
Description: [2018 reprint]. | Providence, Rhode Island: American Mathematical Society, 2018. | Originally published: Princeton, N.J.: Princeton University Press, 2009. Reprinted with corrections by American Mathematical Society, 2018.
Identifiers: LCCN 2018026735 | ISBN 9781470448387 (alk. paper)
Subjects: LCSH: Mathematicians—Portraits. | Mathematicians—Biography. | AMS: History and biography—History of mathematics and mathematicians—Contemporary. msc
Classification: LCC TR681.M38 C66 2018 | DDC 779/.951—dc23 LC record available at https://lccn.loc.gov/2018026735

Copying and reprinting. Individual readers of this publication, and nonprofit libraries acting for them, are permitted to make fair use of the material, such as to copy select pages for use in teaching or research. Permission is granted to quote brief passages from this publication in reviews, provided the customary acknowledgment of the source is given.

Republication, systematic copying, or multiple reproduction of any material in this publication is permitted only under license from the American Mathematical Society. Requests for permission to reuse portions of AMS publication content are handled by the Copyright Clearance Center. For more information, please visit www.ams.org/publications/pubpermissions.

Requests for translation rights and licensed reprints should be sent to reprint-permission@ams.org.

Copyright © 2009 by Mariana Cook.
All rights reserved.

Reprinted with corrections by the American Mathematical Society, 2018.

Printed in Italy.

The paper used in this book is acid-free and falls within the guidelines established to ensure permanence and durability.

Visit the AMS home page at http://www.ams.org/

10 9 8 7 6 5 4 3 2 1   23 22 21 20 19 18

contents

PREFACE MARIANA COOK /page 7

INTRODUCTION ROBERT CLIFFORD GUNNING /page 8

MATHEMATICIANS PORTRAITS /page 11

AFTERWORD BRANDON FRADD /page 197

LIST OF MATHEMATICIANS /page 198

PREFACE MARIANA COOK

**Beauty is truth, truth beauty,— that is all
Ye know on earth, and all ye need to know.**
John Keats, "Ode on a Grecian Urn"

Mathematicians are exceptional. They are not like everyone else. They may look like the rest of us, but they are not the same. For starters, most of them are a great deal smarter. A mathematician has the capacity to perceive the world abstractly at a remarkable level of sophistication, often moving dozens of what they call "mathematical objects" around in their heads for years while working on a single problem.

Truth is the ultimate authority in mathematics. A theorem must be proven to be true. Often, after a decade of work, a proof will only be a page long. It will be beautiful in its simplicity. I have photographed many people: artists, writers, and scientists, among others. In speaking about their work, mathematicians use the words "elegance," "truth," and "beauty" more than everyone else combined.

Mathematicians are bound by fairness. Anyone who solves an outstanding problem with a pencil and piece of paper (regardless of age, race, nationality, or economic circumstance) can be catapulted into the upper echelons of the mathematical community overnight. Unlike with the scientist, a laboratory is not required to do the work. Mathematics may well be the most democratic of creative pursuits, as is the recognition of success by fellow mathematicians. Honesty and conscience are the tools of character required. The work of the mathematician transcends political bounds.

One of the last mathematicians I photographed for this project is one of the youngest in the book, Maryam Mirzakhani. I interviewed her, and after asking general questions about her initial interest in mathematics, I asked her more specifically about her work. She looked at me quizzically, trying to determine how much I might understand of what she could say. I was touched by her consideration. Then she picked up a cup on her desk and began to talk about the shape of its handle, how that shape could be changed, and what mathematical questions and answers could be raised in the process. Delighted to understand a little bit of it, I told her that another mathematician I'd photographed, Dennis Sullivan, had picked up his cup and explained topology to me in exactly the same way. "He's my mathematical grandfather!" she exclaimed. In case you're wondering, Curt McMullen is the link. There is a notable kinship among mathematicians. Students are appreciative of the time and effort given them by their professors, and in turn, they nurture the next generation.

At age twelve, my daughter asked me if I thought there could be another galaxy in which life as we know it exists. I told her I thought there could be. And, if it ever comes to pass, there is one thing about which I have utmost certainty: the thinking individuals who will be able to communicate between galaxies will be the mathematicians. Why? Because they have developed a language of notation to represent ideas that try to explain truths. Where are we in the universe? How do you measure distance and area that morph into other forms? How can you determine the shape of a drum from its sound? Does infinity exist? The actual language of notation will not be the same, but the "mathematicians" in each galaxy will be able to see patterns in one another's language. They will decipher symbols and soon they will exchange ideas with a respect for their mutual effort to understand. As for the rest of us, well, lots of luck!

INTRODUCTION ROBERT CLIFFORD GUNNING

Mathematics is one of the greatest human accomplishments. It has long been an important human activity, from its early use in surveying and in construction in Babylonian and ancient Egyptian times, through the present phenomenal expansion of its use and study. By the period in which Greek mathematics flourished, it was not just important for its uses but it was also a major intellectual endeavor, and already it had developed the abstraction and rigor that continue to be a principal characteristic.

One of the striking aspects of mathematics is its cumulative nature; it is perhaps the only truly cumulative human activity. The axiomatic approach familiar from Euclidean geometry, and indeed the body of geometry the Greeks developed, remain essential parts of mathematics today. Euclid's proof that there are infinitely many prime numbers and the recognition by Pythagoras that π is irrational are as valid now as ever and are still the standard results taught to young students of mathematics. The method of calculating volumes by slicing, as developed by Archimedes, was extended and included in Cavalieri's principle, applying the tools of calculus developed by Newton and Leibniz to the same problems. That method was extended further to Fubini's theorem when the more general theories of measure and integration, developed by Lebesgue and others early in the twentieth century, provided new and more powerful tools for the calculation.

The ancient Greeks appreciated the anomalous nature of the parallel postulate and had begun research on the true nature of that postulate; this research was continued through the development of non-Euclidean geometry in the nineteenth century and the more extensive development of differential geometry since then. This cumulative nature, the fact that nothing once proved is really lost, although much may be forgotten from time to time, means that the body of mathematics is amazingly extensive. The only way in which the mass of results developed over the years can be recalled and understood effectively is by combining a vast number of individual results and observations into a more general, and more abstract, structure that can be grasped and used as a tool for further work. And these abstract tools, when they too are extended and analyzed by continuing research, in turn only can be recalled and understood effectively by combining them in even more abstract and general structures.

This extensive and cumulative nature of mathematics does mean that it is difficult to convey to nonmathematicians a good deal of the true nature of modern mathematics. Of course everyone uses and understands a good deal of mathematics. Business and commerce and construction and so many other fundamental activities rely on mathematical tools to be useful or even to work at all, and some of these mathematical tools themselves can be quite abstract and general, even if the abstraction and generality are effectively hidden by being embedded in computers and electronics. The charm and true fun of mathematics are familiar to anyone who is fascinated by Sudoku or Rubik's Cube. Easily stated puzzles such as the Catalan conjecture (that $1 = 9 - 8 = 3^2 - 2^3$ is the only instance of two nontrivial powers of integers that differ by 1) or Fermat's last theorem (that the equation $x^n + y^n = z^n$ has no nontrivial integer solutions when n is an integer strictly greater than 2) also indicate the intriguing and delightful possibilities in mathematics, even when the solutions of these puzzles can vary from being rather tricky and not altogether obvious to being quite extraordinarily difficult. However, it is very hard to convey a true appreciation of the absolutely fascinating and absorbing beauty of mathematics, the grandeur of its structures, the delight in recognizing what common elements really underlie a number of puzzles, and the joy of completing an extremely involved and challenging calculation and of being the first to do so or the first to come up with a new and significant mathematical structure. A deep appreciation of mathematics really requires an understanding that can come only by knowing enough of the vast structure of mathematics to be able to follow the proofs and arguments. Imagine the difficulty in teaching a true appreciation of music if the only way to enjoy the late quartets was the way Beethoven himself did, by hearing them in his mind after reading the scores as written. Even to convey the significance of some of the problems that guide current research in mathematics—such as the Clay Mathematical Institute's seven Millennium Prize Problems, each of which has a million-dollar reward for the first accepted and published solution—is challenging. Books have been written to give an indication of the nature of the Poincaré conjecture, a characterization of three-dimensional spheres, the first Millennium Prize Problem with an apparent solution and one that at least can be described vaguely in everyday terms; any description of some of the others, like the Hodge conjecture or the Navier–Stokes equation or the Birch and Swinnerton-Dyer conjecture, really requires a considerable background to appreciate, if not even to understand.

That does not mean, though, that mathematicians have given up attempts to explain the nature and joys of mathematics to everyone else in the world. Courses in "mathematical appreciation" or on "mathematics for poets" are common in many universities, and indeed are quite popular in some; but even those do require a level of commitment and work that is more than can be expected from many people in such busy and challenging times as the present. Mathematical puzzles and puzzle books abound, and popular accounts of particular mathematical topics appear with great regularity but often involve only a vague and superficial understanding of what really is going on.

This book is intended to provide another approach to spread more widely an appreciation of the nature of mathematics through an idea that occurred to Brandon Fradd and that he has effectively pushed through to completion. Even as an undergraduate mathematics major at Princeton University in the 1980s, he was concerned with the ways in which mathematics is taught, both to prospective mathematicians and to the general population. When he came across the elegant book of photographs of scientists by Mariana Cook, he conceived the plan of creating a comparable book focused on mathematicians, containing both photographs of current practitioners of mathematics and some brief descriptions of their lives, thoughts, and motivations to do mathematics. In Ms. Cook he found a superb photographer who could not only create perceptive records of the individuals she talked to but could also bring out some of the aspects of their personalities that might indicate the sort of people who find mathematics an overwhelming delight and challenge and what motivates them in this really rather arduous and compelling activity. The result of this collaboration is the current volume. It focuses on some ninety-two mathematicians around the world who have pursued a wide variety of mathematics with an equally wide variety of motivations and gives not only a photographic study of each, but also some indication, in the words of each, of what drives them to do mathematics. The selection is not intended as a list of the "top" current mathematicians but rather is somewhat random. The project began with some of the mathematicians who were Brandon Fradd's teachers and friends at Princeton and expanded with suggestions from those individuals of others throughout the world who could convey a sense of the variety of people who currently practice mathematics. The hope of its creators is that this book might be a way of indicating that the pursuit of mathematics is a continuing activity that attracts a wide variety of delightful, individualistic, and devoted men and women, and might give at least some indication of what motivates and inspires these mathematicians.

MATHEMATICIANS

EDWARD NELSON

Analysis, probability, mathematical physics, logic
Professor of Mathematics, Princeton University

I had the great good fortune to be the youngest of four sons with a seven-year gap between my brothers and me, born into a warm and loving family. This was in Georgia, in the depths of the Depression, where my father organized interracial conferences. He was the sixth Methodist minister in lineal descent. While driving he would amuse himself by mentally representing the license plate numbers of cars as the sum of four squares.

I attended first grade in fascist Italy and still have the notebook in which I wrote to dictation, "Mussolini ama i bambini." What a boon it was to know already in first grade that most of the things I was being taught simply were not so. My mother's skepticism for abstraction led in the same direction.

When I was twelve I took a new deck of cards and idly reordered it: top, bottom, top, bottom, and so forth. I naively asked myself whether the cards would ever return to the same order if I repeated this sufficiently often, and if so how many reorderings would be required. Then I asked the same question for a deck of any number of cards and plotted the results. The graph fluctuated wildly between a regular logarithmic curve below and a straight line above. By the time I was fourteen I had a formula that seemed to work, and a year later I had a proof that it did.

Why do mathematicians work, possibly for years, on a problem? It may be important for applications or for furthering mathematics; it may bring recognition; combined with teaching, it may provide an income—being paid for what one loves to do. But all of these are secondary and the battle against infinite formlessness is the primary reward. Only the joy of making love surpasses the joy of doing mathematics, with skiing a distant third.

Much of my early work was in mathematical physics. I was, and still am, unsatisfied by the orthodox interpretation of quantum mechanics and I invented a theory, stochastic mechanics, with a more concrete interpretation of the Schrödinger equation. By the efforts of many people, this led to some exciting mathematics but it did not meet my hopes for finding a realistic interpretation of quantum theory. This remains a great puzzle.

Then my work took a different turn, and it came through teaching. I was giving a graduate course on probability theory and I wanted to use a heuristic equation involving infinitesimals for the Brownian motion process. Now, in writing papers, one does not need to fill in all the details, but graduate students are more demanding. They want to know just what is going on. I was aware that Abraham Robinson had invented something called nonstandard analysis that made infinitesimals rigorous, so the next semester I gave a course on the subject to learn it and invented a new approach called internal set theory. This theory had the unsettling feature that not all the numbers were what one had always imagined them to be, namely standard. I was hooked. I began to question the most fundamental assumptions of mathematics and became increasingly skeptical as to the consistency of current mathematical practice. The problem is with the acceptance of the notion of completed infinity. There is no evidence in all of creation that God chose to make a completed infinity. The notion is a human fabrication, and there are unsuspected technical problems with it in mathematics. My joyful task is trying to show that contemporary mathematics is indeed inconsistent.

ANDREI OKOUNKOV

Representation theory, algebraic geometry, mathematical physics
Fields Medal
Professor of Mathematics, Princeton University

I find mathematics amazing. Why should numbers capture our world much better than words? Why do such a variety of people, like astronomers, bakers, conductors, and those who make Z-bosons, rely on numbers to get things working exactly right? I am not a philosopher. I simply observe with amazement how the most abstract and cryptic symbols from our notepads and computer screens correspond perfectly with the world around us: with how the rainbows form, how the planets orbit, how everything else happens. Part of the miracle is that math problems, however complicated, always have to work out somehow. Often the outcome is anticipated, sometimes it is a genuine surprise, but never a dead end, a contradiction. Is it because mathematics mirrors the world that exists, or does the world exist because math works out? Luckily, it is not my job to answer this question.

The power of math is that the whole world revolves around the same mathematics. It is the lingua franca of all exact sciences, and once you understand how it works in one particular instance, you can go on and apply the same essential math to millions of other things. You can distill it from one source and use it to infuse or illuminate anything you like. There is an interesting passage to roughly the same effect in Mayakovski's *How to Make Verse*; I recall being impressed by it when I was a teenager. And to continue the parallel with poetry, I think mathematics requires imagination more than any other ingredient. Some particular example, a specific computation, may contain a grain of an important universal mathematical truth. But to recognize it, you need to be able to step back from the formulas, or rather, let your imagination carry you over them. This ability to see big in small, general in specific (like an oak in an acorn), is one of the main qualifications of a mathematician.

And like poetry, math means a lot of hard work, the results of which are not guaranteed. Wonderful math is scarce and precious. We only have a few really good ideas during our careers. Often our memory preserves the exact circumstances in which a particularly good idea surfaced in our heads! We are not like chefs who can produce something delightful every day. This difficulty, this challenge certainly adds to the thrill of a mathematical discovery, but I don't think it is what really drives mathematics. For me, it is minor compared with the importance of better understanding our world. And it is very fortunate that, unlike people who dig for gold, mathematicians can freely share their precious treasures with everybody. Once you understand something really well, it feels great to explain it to all.

MICHAEL ARTIN

Algebraic geometry

Professor of Mathematics, Massachusetts Institute of Technology

When I was nearly forty years old I had a revelation: a recurring dream that I'd had since age twelve was an allegory of my birth! In the dream, I was stuck in a secret passage in our house but eventually worked my way out and emerged into a sunlit cupola. After my revelation, I stopped having the dream.

My mother says that I was a big baby and it was a difficult birth, although I don't know what I weighed. The conversion from German to English pounds adds 10 percent, and I suspect that my mother added another 10 percent every few years. She denies this of course. Anyway, I'm convinced that a birth injury caused my left-handedness and some seizures, which, fortunately, are under control.

The name "Artin" comes from my great-grandfather, an Armenian rug merchant who moved to Vienna in the nineteenth century. Armenians were declared "Aryan" by the Nazis, but one side of my mother's Russian family was Jewish, and because of this, my father Emil was "retired" from the university in Hamburg. We came to America in 1937, when I was three years old.

My father was a great mathematician, and he loved teaching as much as I do. He taught me many things: sometimes mathematics, but also the names of wild flowers. We played music and examined pond water. If there was a direction in which he pointed me, it was toward chemistry. He never suggested that I should follow in his footsteps, and I never made a conscious decision to become a mathematician.

I had decided to study science when I began college, but fields such as chemistry and physics gradually fell away, until biology and mathematics were the only ones left. I loved them both but decided to major in mathematics. I told myself that changing out of mathematics might be easier, since it was at the theoretical end of the science spectrum, and I planned to switch to biology at age thirty when, as everyone knew, mathematicians were washed up. But by then I was too involved with algebraic geometry. My decision to work in that field was made partly because of the dynamic personality of my PhD advisor, Oscar Zariski. I made a lucky choice. Thanks to the influence of Alexander Grothendieck, the field blossomed in the next years, and I have worked there ever since.

JOHN HORTON CONWAY

Group theory, number theory, geometry, combinatorics, game theory

John von Neumann Professor of Applied and Computational Mathematics and Professor of Mathematics, Princeton University

I was born in Liverpool, England in late 1937. My father was a lab assistant in a big Liverpool school that two of the Beatles went to. My father was very knowledgeable about science, and was also very interested in poetry. At home he'd stride up and down, sometimes naked, reciting poetry as he shaved. He was a strange character, an interesting person, I think. My father was also an air-raid warden. Once in a while, the sirens would sound. The war ground itself into me when I was a kid. Sometimes kids wouldn't come to school and we'd learn that their house got bombed and they'd been killed. I was evacuated for a time to Wales. The evacuation scheme for children never worked because their mothers wanted them too much so eventually they returned. I gather at one time I spoke Welsh.

When I entered a new school at age eleven, I had an interview with the headmaster. He asked me what I wanted to do with my life and I told him I wanted to read mathematics at Cambridge. That's what I did seven years later. While I was at that school, I was just as interested in the sciences. I'd always been first, second, or third in every subject, but when puberty hit me, I couldn't care less. I hung around with the kids who weren't interested in anything, the back-of-the-class types, because they were interesting characters. (I've had that trouble ever since. I like interesting characters.) I began to fail and eventually one of the teachers gave me a talking to and I turned around and became top again, particularly in the sciences. I climbed up the academic ladder at Cambridge, and became Fellow of the Royal Society. Shortly after that, Princeton offered me a job and I've been here for twenty-one years.

Among the scientific community, I'm best known for the Game of Life, which opened the field of cellular automata. I have also discovered various huge symmetry groups. It was quite difficult to do and it was a very interesting subject at the time. I am proudest, though, of discovering a whole new world of numbers, which Donald Knuth named "surreal numbers." I wish I'd invented that name. More than a century ago, a great German mathematician, Georg Cantor, discovered the theory of infinite numbers. Two thousand years ago, Archimedes founded the theory of real numbers that we normally use. The surreal numbers include both. Some of them are infinite and are equal to Cantor's numbers. Some of them are equal to the real numbers but there are also mixes of them and infinitesimal numbers. When I discovered them, I went around in a permanent daydream for six weeks thinking about how the explorer Hernando Cortez looked out over the Pacific and saw a world that no Westerner had ever seen before. Nobody had ever seen what I saw before. Although it was totally abstract, it was very real. Abstract things can be real. Numbers can be more real than physical objects. It was an amazing new world of numbers that I discovered, more than numbers.

There was a time in my late twenties when I was rather depressed because I'd gotten a job at Cambridge University very easily and yet I felt I hadn't done enough to justify it. Then I made various discoveries one after another, the first being the "big groups" that the technical mathematician thinks are my best work. In very short order, I discovered the "life game" and the surreal numbers. After a little time, it seemed that everything I touched turned to gold, whereas a few years earlier, nothing I touched turned to anything.

It's a funny thing that happens with mathematicians. What's the ontology of mathematical things? How do they exist? In what sense do they exist? There's no doubt that they do exist but you can't poke and prod them except by thinking about them. It's quite astonishing and I still don't understand it, having been a mathematician all my life. How can things be there without actually being there? There's no doubt that 2 is there or 3 or the square root of omega. They're very real things. I still don't know the sense in which mathematical objects exist, but they do. Of course, it's hard to say in what sense a cat is out there, too, but we know it is, very definitely. Cats have a stubborn reality but maybe numbers are stubborner still. You can't push a cat in a direction it doesn't want to go. You can't do it with a number either. I'm only using the word "number" because you'll have a vague idea in your head as to what I mean. The objects that a mathematician studies are more abstract than numbers but very real.

I often think of cats. I think of trees. I think of dogs occasionally but I don't think of them all that much because dogs are agreeable. They do what you want them to do to some extent. Some people believe that mathematics is what we think it is and it's created by our thoughts. I don't. I'm a Platonist at heart, although I know there are very great difficulties with that view.

FRIEDRICH HIRZEBRUCH

Topology, differential geometry, complex analysis

Professor of Mathematics, University of Bonn, and former Director, Max Planck Institute for Mathematics, Bonn

I was born on October 17, 1927 in Hamm, a town north of the Ruhr district in Germany. My father was the director of a secondary school and taught mathematics. Very early, my interest in numbers arose, and in school, my favorite subject was mathematics. I had good teachers, but I extended my knowledge by studying the mathematical books of my father and by talking to him.

In 1937, I had to join the Deutsches Jungvolk. I was aware of the pogrom of 1938. My father said to his children, "Always remember that I do not agree with this." I did not know that of my beloved authors, Hans Rademacher had left Germany in 1933 and Otto Toeplitz had lost his professorship in Bonn. He escaped to Jerusalem in early 1939, where he died in 1940.

In March of 1945, I became a soldier and in April a prisoner of war, surviving in the meadows along the Rhine, always under the open sky in rain and sunshine, scribbling mathematics on toilet paper, the only paper available. I was released in July 1945. All my family survived, but our house had been destroyed by bombing.

To receive ration cards, I had to clean the British barracks. But on the first day, a British officer asked me in fluent German what I was doing there and what I actually wanted to do. I said, "Mathematics!" He put me in his jeep and drove me home: "Study mathematics!" I did. To this day, I regret that I did not ask for his name.

In November 1945, I began to study mathematics and physics at the nearby University of Münster. The city and the university had been heavily damaged. The only lecture hall left was used for mathematics once every three weeks. Otherwise we had to do exercises at home. The study conditions improved fast. My teachers were Heinrich Behnke (complex analysis) and Heinrich Scholz (mathematical logic). I enjoyed my position as Heinrich Scholz's student assistant, but my heart preferred the more down-to-earth complex analyis. Thanks to Behnke, I received a fellowship to the Eidgenössische Technische Hochschule in Zürich from 1949 to 1950. I thoroughly learned topology from my teachers, Heinz Hopf and Beno Eckmann. I received my doctoral degree in Münster in the summer of 1950. My future wife—also a mathematics student—and I danced during the party after the examinations. During that party it became clear to me that we should marry, and we did so in Princeton in 1952. The marriage is my haven.

After two good years as scientific assistant in Erlangen, I became a member of the Institute for Advanced Study in Princeton from 1952 to 1954. These were the formative years of my mathematical career. Under the influence of several brilliant mathematicians in Princeton and Paris, I learned new mathematical theories from topology, analysis, and algebraic geometry, which finally were combined into my Riemann–Roch theorem. The Princeton results were the reason for the offer of a professorship at Bonn University. I began to work in Bonn in June of 1956 and have been there ever since.

I was so enthusiastic about Princeton that I wanted to have an institute in Germany similar to the School of Mathematics of the Institute for Advanced Study. I began by inviting visiting professors. In 1957, the first meeting of the annual Arbeitstagung took place. Very often Michael Atiyah, with whom I have nine joint papers, was the first speaker. In 1969 the University of Bonn successfully applied to the German Science Foundation for a Special Research Area (SFB) in theoretical mathematics. From then on we had many visitors from all over the world working in the direction they wanted, cooperating and interacting with each other. An SFB has a limited lifetime. But the Arbeitstagungen and SFB were so successful that the senate of the Max Planck Society decided in 1981 to found a Max Planck Institute for Mathematics in Bonn (MPI) to take over the activities of the Arbeitstagung and SFB. We have approximately sixty visitors at any given moment. I was director of the MPI until my retirement in October 1995. The MPI flourishes and I enjoy going there regularly.

JÁNOS KOLLÁR

Algebraic geometry
Professor of Mathematics, Princeton University

My life as a mathematician started—as for many others who grew up in East Europe—with the high school mathematics olympiads. Starting seriously in ninth grade, the best mathematics students compete with others to solve problems. First in their own towns, then against the others in their county, and at the end they can test their skills at an international competition. Everyone has four hours to work on three hard problems. Usually, only the best can solve more than one of them. I was an undistinguished student before, and it was quite a surprise when I did well at these competitions in the ninth grade. Although I had always liked math, this is when I became a devoted mathematician. Until the end of high school, my favorite times were the biweekly meetings on Saturday afternoons when fifty of the best mathematics students came together to work on math problems, to learn, and to grow together. The competition, the challenge, and the excitement were exhilarating.

Facing such challenges is still the main interest for me in research. To me mathematics is the most romantic of all sciences. In my childhood my favorites were the stories of those heroes who went out alone against the unknown: the travels of Marco Polo or Roald Amundsen and the fictional trials of Ivanhoe or Old Shatterhand in the Winnetou novels. The vicarious excitement of these stories is recreated weekly in mathematical research. In mathematics, you do not need expensive equipment or hundreds of assistants. You are up against the unknown alone, succeeding or failing on your own wit. Fortunately for me, with a bad back it is much easier to wield a pen than a sword.

Most of research is just long, slow work and it is hard to know if it leads anywhere. Sometimes, when this quest for new theorems is not going well, I meditate on the Auden line "To fresh defeats he still must move" and go on. Then, finally, if the work is succeeding, I am frequently reminded of a short poem of Browning:

> *Round the cape of sudden came the sea,*
> *And the sun looked over the mountain's rim:*
> *And straight was a path of gold for him,*
> *And the need of a world of men for me.*

Finding unexpected beauties in mathematics and sharing them with others—what can be better?

RICHARD EWEN BORCHERDS

Number theory, lattices, automorphic forms
Fields Medal
Professor of Mathematics, University of California, Berkeley

As a child I played chess seriously but gave it up because I wasn't as good at it as I would have liked to be. In high school my favorite subject was mathematics. But high school mathematics is not very interesting, so I started to read books about mathematics on my own, such as G. H. Hardy and Edward Wright's *The Theory of Numbers.*

One question which endlessly puzzles me is why mathematics exists at all. This is probably one of those ultimate questions—such as, why does the universe exist? Or, what is consciousness?—that may never have any meaningful answer. For example, the axioms for a group are short and natural, taking less than a line to write down and accounting for the natural notion of the symmetries of things. Yet somehow hidden behind these axioms is the monster simple group, a huge and extraordinary mathematical object, which appears to rely on numerous bizarre coincidences to exist. The axioms for groups give no obvious hint that anything like this exists. In fact it took over a century of study of these axioms before the existence of the monster simple group, a huge and extraordinary mathematical object, the largest of the exceptional simple groups, was discovered. It is as if one started to explore a small muddy hole in the ground and found after following difficult narrow passages for several miles that it eventually opened out into a vast cavern whose walls were covered with crystals. The monster group obviously has some sort of independent existence, in the sense that small brown furry creatures from Alpha Centauri will also discover it and agree with us about properties such as its size. This is one way to distinguish good science and knowledge from bad: an advanced civilization on Alpha Centauri will have equivalent forms of general relativity, Galois theory, and so on, but it seems unlikely to me that they have anything resembling postmodernism or our religious stories. I'm not sure what they would make of Mozart. However, seeing the way that such mathematical objects fit together so well sometimes gives me a spooky feeling that they were somehow constructed by some being.

I don't think "intelligent design" has yet picked up on this argument, but for the record I would like to point out my invention of the "stupid design theory": the universe did indeed have a creator, but a rather incompetent and indifferent one.

I prefer to avoid mainstream mathematics research and work on my own. One problem with this is that the most productive areas are (almost by definition) part of mainstream research and the remaining areas are usually rather barren. My own research reminds me of someone picking over a large junkyard trying to find something valuable that has been overlooked by all the other scavengers. Every now and then one finds a new diamond, but most of the time anything one examines closely is yet another piece of junk.

DAVID MUMFORD

Algebraic geometry, artificial intelligence
Fields Medal
University Professor of Applied Mathematics, Brown University

In my own experience, mathematics in general and pure mathematics in particular has always seemed like secret gardens, special places where I could try to grow exotic and beautiful theories. You need a key to get in, a key that you earn by letting mathematical structures turn in your head until they are as real as the room you are sitting in. My father's mother had the gift: she was one of the first women to beat most of the men in the Mathematics Tripos at Cambridge. My aunt also had it: she called the complex numbers a "delightful fiction" when she, too, read maths at Cambridge.

I was born in Three Bridges, Sussex, England, but came to the United States at age three to live with my mother's family on Long Island Sound, where later my father worked for the newly created United Nations. My mother and her father also encouraged me in science. They both loved astronomy, and I ground my own lens for a reflecting telescope to see sunspots, craters on the moon, and the planets. But I was not a natural with physical devices, and my homemade relay-based computer self-destructed when a spark lit its paper tape of instructions. At Harvard I finally met real mathematicians talking about things like "rings" (abstract algebraic structures that have nothing to do with your fingers) and "barreled spaces" (infinite dimensional geometries where functions become points)—a secret garden indeed.

Professionally, I have had two passions. The pure one is algebraic geometry and within it, moduli spaces. Algebraic geometry is the creation of Pierre de Fermat and René Descartes: the study of loci (called "varieties") in Euclidean spaces defined by polynomial equations. Moduli spaces are particular varieties that serve as maps describing all the other objects in the whole field, the other varieties. You choose particular classes of varieties, such as elliptic curves: then the set of all these curves, up to isomorphism, form the points of one of these moduli spaces. The moduli spaces then are special, very central spaces in the theory, like the index to a book. Forcing them to reveal their intrinsic properties was my goal.

My other passion is applying mathematics to artificial intelligence (AI), specifically finding the right mathematical approach for describing thought. This is a quest littered with false starts and failed "breakthroughs," but my candidate for doing this is Bayesian statistics, and I have worked hard to find models for visual perception using these ideas. In applied math, you must always worry whether you are paying attention to the data or whether you are forcing reality into a mathematical straitjacket. But, naturally, I am convinced my choice is the right one. Plato said, "The sparks that paint the sky . . . can be apprehended only by reason and thought," but new experiments have a habit of overturning old theories.

It is said nowadays that a large proportion of all successful scientists and artists have a touch of Asperger's syndrome. Perhaps this is what they need to focus so narrowly on their work. But its downside is a disconnect with the people and the life around you. To avoid this, a family is what you need. I have been lovingly drawn back into the real world by my first wife, Erika, a poet, with whom we raised a family of four wonderful children; and by my second wife, Jenifer, an artist, whom I married after Erika passed away from cancer. I retired this year and enjoy the amazing good fortune of a large extended family, now with three stepchildren as well as my four children, five children-in-law and twelve grandchildren (please excuse the mathematician for counting so exactly his blessings).

BRYAN JOHN BIRCH

Number theory
Professor Emeritus of Mathematics, University of Oxford

My grandfather was a self-made man who built up a bacon-curing business. At that time, it was the custom that eldest sons went into the family business, so though my father clearly had mathematical ability, there was no question of his going to university. My father was a reluctant but successful and popular employer, but when it came to his turn, he made sure that his children should choose their own careers, and we have all been very grateful.

As a little boy, I always enjoyed sums and my career has been in the theory of numbers. When I was about eight years old, I asked an elderly gentleman what I should do in order to be a mathematician. He told me that he thought mathematicians were often Fellows of Trinity. I had no idea how one might become a Fellow of Trinity, but it seemed to involve passing examinations rather well (which I was certainly good at) and learning a lot of mathematics, which is what I wanted to do anyway. Fortunately I realized quite quickly that it is inappropriate to "learn" mathematics; mathematics is about proof, which means proper understanding of reasons for its propositions to be certain.

In due course, I won a scholarship to Trinity and went up to study for the Mathematical Tripos. It was wonderful: Cambridge is a beautiful place, and for the first time in my life I was working hard doing what I loved best, thinking about mathematics with plenty of like-minded friends of high ability. At the end of my undergraduate course, Ian Cassels agreed to supervise my research. He set me to work on some problems in the geometry of numbers, which I solved without undue difficulty. He also told me to attend Harold Davenport's wonderful seminar in University College London, where I learned the greater pleasure of solving really hard problems. For my thesis on the geometry of numbers, I was elected to a Trinity Prize Fellowship. I guess I had fulfilled my childhood ambition! My training years ended with a year in Princeton, where I learned that mathematics is at its most beautiful when its truths are made to seem natural as well as certain.

If I am remembered, it will be for my share of the Birch–Swinnerton-Dyer conjectures. I got to know Peter Swinnerton-Dyer at the very beginning of my research. Before my Princeton year we wrote one or two joint papers of no great importance, and he taught me to appreciate opera. In Princeton, I read André Weil's beautiful notes reformulating Carl Siegel's work on quadratic forms in terms of a natural "Tamagawa measure" for linear algebraic groups. When I returned, Peter had a job in the fledgling Computer Laboratory. We decided to look at the next natural case, elliptic curves, using the computer to test whether there was any correlation between their local behavior (over finite fields) and their global behavior (over the rational numbers). We were lucky: there was indeed a very precise correspondence, which could be formulated in terms of the zeta functions of the curves. At that time, there was practically nothing known about the analytic theory of such functions, so we had to find out everything for ourselves (in Weil's words, "they had to learn some mathematics"). There turned out to be an incredibly beautiful theory, which is still incomplete. We had the joy of working in a completely fresh area of beautiful mathematics, so beautiful that it was certain to be important. We knew that no one else (except some close friends) had any idea of what we were finding, so we were able to work for three years before publishing.

When we started working together, the arithmetic theory of elliptic and modular functions was unfashionable and of no obvious use, but it was always surpassingly beautiful. Nowadays it is important to the computer security industry, and horribly fashionable. In pure mathematics, aesthetic instinct is the most reliable guide to the value of a piece of research, even if one is primarily interested in possible practical applications.

SIR MICHAEL FRANCIS ATIYAH

Algebraic topology, algebraic geometry
Fields Medal, Abel Prize
Former Master of Trinity College, University of Cambridge; first Director of the Isaac Newton Institute, Cambridge; and Honorary Professor of Mathematics, University of Edinburgh

Many scientists in the twentieth century emerged from complex backgrounds, forced to emigrate by the oppression of Nazi Germany. This enforced cosmopolitanism may have broadened their outlook and helped their subsequent careers. While I was not one of Hitler's refugees, I did oscillate in my childhood between Europe and the Middle East. My mother was Scottish, my father Lebanese, and we lived in Khartoum. My secondary schooling until the age of sixteen was in Egypt, and my grandmother lived in Lebanon.

In 1945 we moved to England and, after my studies in Cambridge, we spent much time in the United States. I find it difficult to answer the question, where do you come from? In a similar way I find equal difficulty when asked, what kind of mathematician are you? I usually evade the question by just saying that I am a geometer in the broad sense, secure in the comfort that "God is a geometer." For me, just as there is only one world, even if parts of it are more familiar than others, so there is only one mathematics. I dislike frontiers, political or intellectual, and I find that ignoring them is an essential catalyst for creative thought. Ideas should flow without hindrance in their natural course.

My own mathematical trajectory started in algebraic geometry and moved in small and natural steps through topology and differential geometry to analysis and ultimately theoretical physics. At every stage this was a very social process, in which close friendships were formed, which broadened my horizons. Fritz Hirzebruch in Bonn was my first colleague and mentor, and his annual Arbeitstagung became a great meeting house for my generation. Jean-Pierre Serre in Paris and Princeton educated me by the clarity and elegance of his thought and exposition.

In Princeton and later at Harvard and MIT, I formed close partnerships with Raoul Bott and Is Singer, who taught me about Lie groups and functional analysis. Back in Oxford I made my first tentative steps into modern physics under the tutelage of my old friend Roger Penrose. This modest incursion subsequently developed into a major preoccupation under the stimulus and guidance of Edward Witten. In subsequent years I was fortunate to attract many brilliant graduate students, some of whom became, eventually, colleagues and collaborators. I learned much from them, realizing at the same time how mathematical taste and skills are a reflection of the personality. Diversity in temperament and outlook is to be welcomed, and creativity flourishes best with a minimum of guidance and a maximum of freedom and encouragement.

Mathematicians are generally thought of as some kind of intellectual machine, a great brain that crunches numbers and spits out theorems. In fact we are, as Hermann Weyl said, more like creative artists. Although strongly constrained by the rules of logic and by physical experience, we use our imagination to make great leaps into the unknown. The development of mathematics over thousands of years is one of the great achievements of civilization. Some mathematicians, most notably G. H. Hardy, gloried in their "purity" and disdained anything useful or applied. I take the opposite view and am extremely pleased if anything I have done turns out to have practical value. More generally, I view mathematics as contributing to science and society and as an integral part of education and learning.

As a result of these views I have always seen it as a responsibility to undertake general roles such as the presidency of the Royal Society, the mastership of Trinity College, Cambridge, or the presidency of Pugwash.* Mathematicians depend ultimately on society for their livelihood and the privilege of working on something that passionately interests them. In return we must, in various ways, repay this debt and encourage our fellow citizens to take a friendly and tolerant view of our strange profession.

---

*Pugwash is an organization of influential scholars and public figures concerned with reducing the danger of armed conflict and seeking cooperative solutions for global problems.

ISADORE MANUAL SINGER

Analysis, differential geometry
Abel Prize
Institute Professor of Mathematics, Massachusetts Institute of Technology

My parents met and married in Toronto, Canada, after emigrating from Poland in 1917. They moved to Detroit, Michigan, where I was born in 1924. I was a bright student, but unfocused. Summers were spent playing baseball and reading. I woke up to the world of science when my high school chemistry teacher introduced me to the elegantly ordered periodic table. Soon I was president of the science club and lecturing on relativity.

I entered the University of Michigan in September 1941, choosing physics over English literature as a major; for me, electromagnetism was easier to understand than poetry. Because of World War II, I rushed through the undergraduate program before being inducted into the U.S. Army Signal Corps in January 1944. The end of the war found me in the mudflats of Luzon, running a Signal Corps school on radio communications for units of the Philippine army. While my fellow officers played poker at night, I was engrossed in two extension courses offered by the University of Chicago, one in differential geometry and the other in group theory. I felt I needed a better background in mathematics to understand my undergraduate courses in relativity and quantum mechanics.

I entered graduate school at the University of Chicago in January of 1947, planning to spend one year in mathematics before returning to physics. But mathematics was so exciting that I stayed put. I didn't know it then, but in the coming decades, high energy theoretical physics would move closer to modern mathematics, and the interface between geometry and physics would eventually become the focus of my scientific career.

As a graduate student, I quickly filled the gaps in my mathematical background and specialized in analysis. S. S. Chern joined the department in 1949 and his course in geometry was fascinating. I think in terms of pictures, not words, and Chern used just the right algebra to describe the pictures of fiber bundles. I spent the next ten years learning differential geometry and with my MIT colleague, Warren Ambrose, modernized Chern's approach to it.

In 1962, Sir Michael Atiyah and I discovered and proved the Index theorem. It gives a formula for the number of solutions to certain differential equations in terms of the geometry and topology of the surrounding space. A key example was Dirac's equation for the spinning electron. The theorem and its proof brought together analysis, geometry, and topology in unexpected ways. Many classical formulas turned out to be special cases of the Index theorem. Atiyah and I extended our results in diverse directions. In the last thirty years mathematicians and physicists have added much to index theory and found applications to high energy physics.

In the mid-1970s it became clear that the geometry of fiber bundles in mathematics was the same as gauge theories in physics, fundamental to the description of elementary particles and their interactions. In 1977, I started a seminar in math/physics because I wanted to understand how physicists quantized the geometry I knew so well and why they wanted to do so. New discoveries connecting mathematics with physics have insured the continued vitality of the seminar.

Beyond math, teaching and public service have been an important part of my academic career. From 1970 to 2000, I served on several committees in Washington, D.C., advising the federal government and explaining to the public the importance of science for our national welfare. I was a member of the White House Science Council during the Reagan administration and chairman of the National Academy of Science's Committee on Science and Public Policy, an experience that considerably broadened my view of science and of the people involved in both its funding and creation.

I am now in my eighties, and my passion for mathematics and its applications has never diminished. That nature is mathematical is awesome. Maybe some day we will understand the brain well enough to explain that mystery. In the meantime, I continue to scribble on a yellow pad trying to bring my own geometric insights to the puzzles of physics.

MIKHAEL LEONIDOVICH GROMOV

Geometric group theory, differential geometry

Jay Gould Professor of Mathematics, Courant Institute of Mathematical Sciences, New York University, and Professor, Institut des Hautes Études Scientifiques

The imprint of the world in our minds is not photographic; all the brain knows of the outside world is a chaotic sequence of electric impulses and out of these it creates a structural entity: our perception of what we see and hear. Most of the time, an adult's brain talks to itself and creates more and more refined structures within itself. The word "structure" means a mathematical structure, something which becomes more and more abstract and better and better logically organized in the course of this self-conversation. The mathematical ability of each person's brain by far exceeds those of the greatest geniuses of all time. Nobody, given the input the brain starts with, could be able to arrive at such a level of abstraction, for instance, as the five-fold symmetry (for example, a starfish), which you, or rather your brain, recognizes instantaneously regardless of a particular size, shape, or color of an object.

And then, at some point, this process of creation of structures by the brain gets in touch with the linguistic part of the brain that generates thoughts that can be perceived and directed by your conscious mind. Here the mathematics starts. Your brain, inherently, is driven for an unknown reason and by an unknown process, to the creation of structures that are abstractions of the inputs the brain receives. When such input reflects the structures already created by the brain from the external world, it starts to analyze these structures within structures. When this process reaches the surface (the tiny fragment of your brain activity which we call consciousness), it becomes mathematics.

We are all fascinated with structural patterns: periodicity of a musical tune, a symmetry of an ornament, self-similarity of computer images of fractals. And the structures already prepared within ourselves are the most fascinating of all. Alas, most of them are hidden from ourselves. When we can put these structures-within-structures into words, they become mathematics. They are abominably difficult to express and to make others understand. Think of a village of deaf people where the music is communicated by writing down musical scores. Little by little you learn how to hear music written in scores and your brain listening to it receives a fantastic treat; then the brain demands more and more of it. Brains are our masters, with only 2 percent of our body weight, they take 20 percent of the oxygen resources of our bodies; you cannot resist their commands. You become a mathematician, a slave of this insatiable hunger of your brain, of everybody's brain, for making structures of everything that goes into it.

KEVIN DAVID CORLETTE

Lie groups, differential geometry
Professor of Mathematics, University of Chicago

I became interested in science at an early age, perhaps five or six. I was born into a family with a particular religious outlook, and it became clear to me fairly early on that theirs was not a worldview that suited me well. However, it still had a considerable grip on my imagination, and I decided that I needed some kind of counterweight to the certainties with which I was being presented. I became interested in science at least partly out of this need. Science was an approach to building certainty about the fundamental nature of the universe that was based on honest exploration and testing of ideas, rather than the (to me) murky foundations of religious faith.

My earliest scientific interests were mainly in chemistry and biology, probably because these seemed most relevant to gaining the kind of control I was looking for over the apparent chaos of life and nature. As I grew older, my interests moved in what I thought of as more fundamental directions: the true nature of matter, space, and time. Mathematics was initially of interest to me primarily as the conceptual instrument used by physics. I began to see mathematics as intrinsically interesting in the eighth grade, when I took Euclidean geometry and found great pleasure in constructing proofs. I think the understanding of a more sophisticated brand of mathematics than I had previously encountered also opened up some hope in me that the sources of certainty could be explored more definitively than I had succeeded in doing thus far. From that time on, my interest in physics and mathematics ran in parallel, until I decided in college that I wanted to be a mathematician.

I went to graduate school at Harvard in the 1980s and studied with mathematicians such as Raoul Bott and Clifford Taubes. My imagination was captured by the torrent of ideas surrounding gauge theory and symplectic geometry at that time. For a while, I worked on something called the Hitchin–Kobayashi conjecture but didn't make much progress. (It was eventually resolved by Simon Donaldson and, independently, by Karen Uhlenbeck and Shing-Tung Yau.) I gave up trying to prove the conjecture but was still fascinated by the general framework which suggested it, involving a relationship between the existence of zeros of moment maps (a notion from symplectic geometry) and the algebro-geometric notion of stability. I found another general example in which such a relationship could be considered, involving flat connections on vector bundles over Riemannian manifolds. I managed to prove the analogue of the Hitchin–Kobayashi conjecture in this setting and only later realized that what I had done could be formulated in the well-known language of harmonic maps. This discovery led in some fascinating directions. One of these was Carlos Simpson's development of a non-Abelian version of Hodge theory for Kaehler manifolds. My theorem provided one half of the correspondence Simpson needed; the other half was found by Simpson himself, in his thesis written at Harvard, at more or less the same time. (Neither of us was aware of what the other was doing at the time.) Another direction was a proof of superrigidity for lattices in certain rank one Lie groups. The phenomenon of superrigidity for lattices in higher rank Lie groups, strengthening the Mostow rigidity, was discovered by Gregory Margulis in the 1970s, but it was clear that entirely new ideas would be needed for the rank one cases in which superrigidity might hold.

It turned out that harmonic maps could be applied to this question but, to match the strength of Margulis's results in higher dimensions, one had to consider harmonic maps with values in spaces with singularities. Mikhael Gromov and Richard Schoen developed such a theory in the 1990s and were able to apply my extension of the Siu–Bochner formula to prove superrigidity for the rank one cases where it was expected to hold. It was remarkable to see the ideas grow in these beautiful and unexpected directions.

SUN-YUNG ALICE CHANG

Geometric analysis

Professor of Mathematics, Princeton University

I was born in China in the ancient capital city of Xian. It was during the period of the Chinese Revolution, so my family moved to Hong Kong and then to Taiwan when I was two. My father was an architect and my mother an accountant. I grew up in Taiwan and attended National Taiwan University.

While I was growing up, I was fascinated with Chinese literature but also very good in mathematics. I found mathematics simple and elegant; I enjoyed the logical way of thinking. After World War II, the economic environment in Taiwan was extremely harsh, so it was much easier for young people with backgrounds in science and technology to get good jobs and become independent. I decided to major in mathematics in college partially out of practical considerations. It seems that my undergraduate class of mathematics students was a very special one—of the forty students in the class there were twelve girls. Starting from freshman year, five of us formed a group and we studied and played together. We were the loud group of the class and had a lot of fun. It is only when I attended graduate school at Berkeley that I began to realize that being a woman mathematician can be a lonely experience.

In graduate school at UC Berkeley, my thesis was in classical analysis. Roughly speaking, there are three branches of mathematics: analysis, geometry, and algebra. In analysis, one usually divides things into small pieces; one analyzes each piece individually and then combines the information.

I married one of my classmates during the last year of graduate school. My husband, Paul Yang, is a geometer who views things in terms of shapes and pictures. In the early years of our marriage, we discussed mathematics in a general sense but seldom discussed our own research projects with each other. Gradually, we realized that some of the problems we were working on could be viewed both geometrically and analytically. We began to do joint work together after ten years of marriage! The field we now work in is called geometric analysis, where one uses methods in analysis to handle geometric problems. One of the main problems is to classify a class of four-dimensional manifolds. The problem is intimately related to problems in physics since the world we are living in is three-dimensional, but with the extra dimension of time.

I have always felt that mathematics is a language like music. To learn it systematically, it is necessary to master small pieces and gradually add another piece and then another. In a sense, mathematics is like the classical Chinese language—very polished and very elegant. Sitting in a good mathematics lecture is like sitting in a good opera. Everything comes together. They get to the heart of the problem and I enjoy it!

SHING-TUNG YAU

Differential geometry, partial differential equations
Fields Medal
Professor of Mathematics, Harvard University

I grew up in a village in Hong Kong. It was a beautiful landscape with oxen and other animals. I could see the ocean and the mountains, and I went to school in this farmland in my early years. For my middle years, I went to school in the city. My father was a professor in Chinese philosophy and in economics. A professor didn't earn much money in those days. I learned a lot from him but he died when I was fourteen. We had to struggle because we were a very poor family. I had eight brothers and sisters. My mother had to work very hard and we, in turn, learned to deal with life in a hard way.

I did my undergraduate work in math at the university in Hong Kong. I learned a lot from the professors there but not enough because most teachers did not have a PhD. While in college, I had a professor from Berkeley and he recommended me to Berkeley as a student where I went to study in 1969. There were a lot of antiwar demonstrations and student-movement activity in Berkeley at that time. I studied very hard and I learned a lot. I completed my doctoral work and thesis and graduated in two years. It was a good experience. I began to think about what to do and what was the best subject for me. There were close to one hundred math professors at Berkeley in those days. It was a huge department and there were sixty PhD's the year I graduated.

I am a geometer interested in geometric analysis. When I began, many geometers were not interested in analysis. I felt that it was very important to combine the two subjects together. I use a great deal of nonlinear differential equations to study differential geometry. I'm very interested in mathematical physics and my friends in the physics community have been extremely helpful. I started to work on curvatures in general relativity, which was very fruitful. I solved some important problems in that subject which developed into string theory. In the past fifteen years, I've been working very much with curvatures and how they relate to string theory. A lot of my work is related to physics. I also work on curvatures and how they relate to engineering and computer graphics.

Mathematicians lie somewhere between artists and writers on the one hand and physicists, chemists, and biologists on the other. We try to get natural problems from the physical world, but we also try to create problems based on the development of our understanding of nature. It's like an artist who paints a picture. Some of the pictures are realistic and you see the world. But an artist can also see nature and create an image related to it in an abstract way. We do that, too. I do not try to go too far from nature. Like artists, some go far from the natural world and others do not. There are different tastes for different people.

JOHN FORBES NASH, JR.

Game theory, differential geometry, partial differential equations

Nobel Prize in Economics

Senior Research Mathematician, Princeton University

I was born in a small city in southern West Virginia. My father was an electrical engineer. And there came a time in my life there when I would go into his office and play around with some calculator machines which they happened to have but which were not so common in those days. I developed an early interest in arithmetic and studied some mathematics on my own so I could study higher-level math before I went to college. My parents also arranged for me to study part time in a local junior college while also continuing in the town high school.

I went to Carnegie Mellon as an undergraduate because I had a special scholarship that paid full tuition and was specific for study there. Later I became a graduate student in mathematics at Princeton.

My times of "mental illness" (as it is called) began in 1959. There were intervals of returning to rational thinking but not of much happiness and good adjustment. After an interval like that, I would go back into the delusional thinking, and I came out of it only gradually after many years.

Mathematical thinking is logical and rational thinking. It's not like writing poetry. In general, persons who can work effectively in mathematics must be mostly rational in thinking when doing such work. However, I can guess that one could have very specialized delusions, like some extreme and atypical religious cultic orientation and also be a good mathematician. This seems possible.

Nowadays I am best known for some contributions to game theory. I received the Economics Nobel Memorial Prize for that work. It's not a prize in mathematics although my work was mathematical. It used a very central theorem in topology, the Brouwer fixed point theorem. That's a theorem that has a particular topological or geometrical character. It has to do with space but the space could be of various dimensions.

Currently I have a few areas of research that particularly interest me: game theory, spacetime and general relativity, and mathematical logic are among these. There are some mathematicians who are problem solvers specifically. And there are people who are theory developers: they may work on very closely related topics over many years in a certain area of mathematics. I haven't been like that. I have been relatively less specialized.

KAREN KESKULLA UHLENBECK

Partial differential equations, gauge theory

Sid W. Richardson Regents Professor of Mathematics, The University of Texas, Austin

It would be easy to say either too little or too much about the past. I was a lucky child, growing up in the optimistic post–World War II climate. We played in the rural hills of northern New Jersey, prepared ourselves for our chance at the great world of culture: art, music, science, and intellect. My mother, an artist, remains a major influence on my life although she has been dead a number of years. Through her I received just about the right amount of introduction to nontraditional life styles and intellectual ambition.

We should remember that a girl did not become a mathematician by doing what was expected of her in suburban New Jersey. I discovered, through my engineer father, the popularized books of physicist George Gamow and astronomer Frederick Hoyle. I wished for myself that my future life would include both the outdoor and science activities. I would have liked to do everything; it is perhaps only accidental that I turned out to be so good at and so in love with mathematics.

I learned about mathematics in my freshman honors course at the University of Michigan. I still remember the thrill of taking limits to compute derivatives, and the little boxes used in proving the Heine–Borel theorem. The structure, elegance, and beauty of mathematics struck me immediately, and I lost my heart to it. I remember in vivid detail the first theorems I understood, and even more so the theorems I proved on my own . . . just like in the textbook, only thought up and invented without sneaking a look at the text. From there, the step to research mathematics has been a small one. I still delight in the minute and private successful arguments, even as the large impersonal complicated structures built on these small ideas continue to fill me with awe.

I have been privileged to be a player in one of the major developments in mathematics of the past thirty years. During this period, the theory and structure of partial differential equations have been used and developed for the purpose of studying geometry. Many of the core ideas come from theoretical physics. It has been an exciting intellectual life. To explain the power and beauty of mathematics to outsiders is difficult. Mathematics takes ideas from the external world and makes them abstract, juggles them around to create structure, and then spews them back with amazingly broad and useful consequences. The best comparison that most of us have is the comparison with musical structure. Many mathematicians are serious musicians.

What does it take to be a mathematician? My experience has been that the key ingredient is the fascination with the theory and the manipulations of its structure. It does not take brilliance, but love of a great game!

I am not so sure I am happy that mathematics is useful. The uses most likely do more harm than good (to quote my mother). I am content with the aesthetic rewards.

JAMES HARRIS SIMONS

Differential geometry
Founder, Renaissance Technologies LLC

I can't remember a time when I wasn't interested in math. I remember calculating all the powers of two when I was quite little. I thought it was horrifying when my father told me a car could run out of gas. I pondered why that should be. I figured all you have to do is just use half of what's remaining. Then you could use half of that and so on. I wasn't especially good at arithmetic. I made arithmetic mistakes, but I knew that math was for me and I tried to move as fast as I could in it. When I got to MIT, I had already taken advanced placement math and started a little bit ahead. Then in the spring of my freshman year, I took a graduate course in algebra because there were no prerequisites except some mathematical sophistication, of which I had none. I struggled through that course, doing the problems but not really understanding. During the summer, something clicked and it all fell into place. In the next year I had the same experience with other advanced subjects: initial confusion, then, after a decent interval, a click.

I graduated from MIT and after receiving my PhD at Berkeley, I taught at MIT and at Harvard. I worked as a mathematician for fifteen years. My father and I also made an investment with some MIT friends in South America. It turned out to be quite successful, but it took a long time. In the meantime, I was busy doing mathematics.

I went on to Princeton and worked as a code-cracker at the time of the Vietnam War. I worked for the Institute for Defense Analysis. It was National Security Agency work and highly classified. The IDA had a policy that permitted you to spend as much as half of your time on your own mathematics. During those four years, I solved the problem called the Plateau problem and the Bernstein conjecture, two different aspects of the same problem. My boss's boss was a man named Maxwell Taylor, who was a famous general and John Kennedy's military adviser. He wrote quite a stupid cover piece in the *New York Times Magazine* about how we were winning the war in Vietnam, and that aggravated me. I wrote a letter to the *Times* saying that not everyone who worked for General Taylor necessarily subscribed to his views. In due course, I was fired.

I needed a job at age twenty-nine. Stony Brook University asked me to be chairman of their mathematics department. I was an aggressive guy, always trying to get new things organized. People knew that about me. I took the job. We built the department, and I worked on mathematics, which led to something known as "the Chern–Simons invariants." I remained active in mathematics, but at a certain point I got very frustrated because I was working on problems I couldn't get anywhere with. At the same time, the South American investment finally paid off some money. Given that, I thought it was time to change careers, and I did.

I went into the investing business without any thought of applying mathematics at all. I had some ideas and they worked out well. After a few years, we began applying mathematics but it was very different from the math that I had been doing. I had spent fifteen years as a pure mathematician doing geometry and topology, very abstract mathematics. I have been in the investment business for thirty years and have used some mathematical methods, but this work is very far afield from the rather deep, abstract thinking that one has to do in the academic world.

Interestingly, the work I did as a code-cracker during the Vietnam War turned out to be extremely useful. As a code-cracker, you see a lot of data from your adversary. You get ideas. You test them. Most of them are wrong. If you're lucky, you get a few hits and you begin to see. It's similar with predicting financial data: you have an idea that when one thing happens, you might expect to see a certain pattern. You can test it out. Maybe you're right. Maybe you're wrong. It's experimental science using mathematical methods but it is not mathematics.

Much of this work is modeling financial markets, in the hope that organizing the data properly will help with predictions of the future, rather the way the solar system was modeled in the days before Isaac Newton. I look at a lot of financial data and try to make mathematical pictures from it; it can be elegant but is quite different from proving theorems. In the last few years I have gone back to doing some pure mathematics. When you work on a mathematical problem you think very deeply about it, shutting yourself off from other things and thinking primarily just about that problem. You get an idea at the oddest times. That is the memorable event, so often happening when you were physically attending to something else, like a dinner party or a movie. Thinking about a mathematical problem insulates you from other things and can be comforting. It feels good. It's fun.

PHILLIP GRIFFITHS

Differential geometry, algebraic geometry
Professor of Mathematics and former Director, Institute for Advanced Study, Princeton

I grew up in rural North Carolina and went to largely rural schools and then Georgia Military Academy near Atlanta. It was a tradition in the South back then to go to military school. That's where I really fell in love with mathematics. After being exposed to the subject by a superb teacher, Lottie Wilson, I was going to think about mathematics no matter what. I went to graduate school in math at Princeton and did a postdoc at Berkeley. I taught at Harvard for many years and then went to Duke University as provost. In 1991, I went to the Institute for Advanced Study in Princeton as director.

There's probably fairly good agreement among the mathematical community when something is a beautiful piece of mathematics. Creativity is not something that you can force. It just has to happen. You work hard, struggle with a problem, get stuck, go off and do something else, and out of the blue, you'll see something. We do mathematics primarily for aesthetic reasons. Physics is also a very beautiful subject but it has to connect with nature. Mathematics is the language of science. The practical side of mathematics permeates our lives, whether it's in security codes or people manipulating markets with exotic financial instruments.

My primary interest has always been geometry. I'm particularly interested in modern geometry, which has to do with topology (the geometry of shape), algebraic geometry (algebraic equations and their pictures and analysis), differential geometry (metric shapes like curved surfaces, soap bubbles, things like that). Even as an administrator, I always spend the first few hours of every day doing mathematics, and I've always had students. I love students. They amaze me. They come into a subject fresh so they think about things differently, and it's really fun to watch them develop.

For the last ten years, I've been working with the World Bank's science and technology programs, primarily in Africa, to try to help them build an indigenous scientific community. Historically, they sent students abroad to study and they wouldn't go back. To bring modern science and engineering to bear on the life in Africa, whether it's agriculture, health care, or the economy, they always had to import experts because their people had emigrated.

Kids are not going into math and science as much as they used to in this country, in Europe, or even in China. They want to go into business. Low- and medium-end innovation, making a widget better or improving a production line, is going on in China and Korea and India. In the United States, there is more emphasis on the creativity that gives you totally new technology: the high-value intellectual property that comes out of science and mathematics. You don't notice a drop-off in the students coming out of MIT and Caltech and Stanford. That will probably remain important here.

Unfortunately, science education, especially math, from kindergarten through twelfth grade is not in a good state now. Even in the better schools, math isn't being taught well. There are math wars between teaching skills like doing fractions or equations versus teaching concepts. The recent textbooks I've seen are just awful compared to the ones that I had. First, they're too big. If you can't say it in about 150 pages, then you don't understand the subject well enough. You have to choose what's most important to explain clearly. If you do it well enough, students can figure out the rest.

Science literacy is extremely important in today's world. Quantitative, analytical skills are necessary in many jobs. Evidence-based reasoning, which is what science teaches you, is where we're breaking down. To be a good citizen in this country, you need to have a general knowledge of science. Look at the evolution debate. Look at the way data is presented to us in the newspapers. Many people don't have the foggiest notion what it means or how to interpret it.

Part of the problem is the teaching. Teachers get into the system primarily through education schools. The emphasis is more on pedagogy than substance. A math teacher, even in elementary school, should have a master's-level understanding of the subject. With that deep an understanding, you're better able to teach elementary material in a simple way. Otherwise, you make it too complicated. My first teacher, Mrs. Wilson, was foremost a talented mathematician, and that's what made her a great teacher.

GANG TIAN

Differential and symplectic geometry, geometric analysis
Professor of Mathematics, Princeton University and Beijing University

My mother was a mathematician. She studied Hilbert's sixteenth problem and made an outstanding contribution. This is a problem of studying a dynamical system governed by two polynomials. When I was a kid, my mother often gave me logic problems to solve. Most of them were not that hard but were very interesting. I liked to think about them. My mother also told me about other things, such as historical stories and Chinese classical poems. When I was seven, the Cultural Revolution started in China and lasted ten years. During that period, universities were essentially closed and my parents went to the countryside. I stayed with my grandparents and enjoyed a lot of free time because schools did not run normally. My classmates and I had a lot of fun working in factories, rice fields, and on playgrounds. My mother got me two old books on Euclidean geometry and elementary algebra. I studied them in my spare time and got fascinated by them. I liked mathematics because of its abstractness, elegance, and neatness. Sometimes it took me a while to figure out how to prove a theorem in Euclidean geometry, but once it was done, I felt I had achieved something and was pleased. But I did not know at this point that I would become a mathematician since the universities were closed and I could not even hope to go to university. I would have felt lucky enough if I could stay in a city and have a job.

In 1977, shortly after the Cultural Revolution ended, universities reopened in China. I was happy and hopeful. After taking two entrance exams, I was admitted into Nanjing University, a top university in China which was near my home. I had a wonderful experience there. I met many friends there and gained a solid mathematical background. I saw more of the beauty of mathematics and decided to continue doing mathematics. In 1982, I went to Beijing University, a famous and distinguished university in China, as a graduate student for a master's degree. I started my mathematical research in analysis there and also studied topics in geometry. In 1984, I went to America to further my study and got my PhD from Harvard University a few years later. Since then, I have been working in geometry and partial differential equations.

I enjoy doing mathematical research. It does not rely on equipment. When I think about mathematical problems, I feel independent and peaceful. If I happen to solve one of them, I have the joy of being successful and able to do something ahead of other people.

One of my research fields is differential geometry. This has a long history. A basic problem in geometry is to understand the role of curvature in the study of spaces. My work involves constructing a nice geometric structure on a given space, i.e., a space whose curvature is more homogeneously distributed in a suitable sense. Such a nice structure can be applied to understanding topology of underlying spaces. To construct this nice structure, I need to develop tools in geometric analysis and nonlinear differential equations. Another part of my research includes symplectic geometry. My collaborators and I construct invariants for symplectic manifolds and apply them to studying symplectic topology and constructing solutions to equations. Construction of these invariants has roots in classical enumerative geometry: through any two points, there is a unique line, through any five points in general position, there is a unique quadratic curve, through any eight points in general position, there are twelve cubic curves. It turns out that these can be extended to any symplectic manifold by counting curves that are solutions of certain differential equations. Furthermore, one can even prove some beautiful relations among these counting numbers.

HEISUKE HIRONAKA

Algebraic geometry
Fields Medal
Professor Emeritus of Mathematics, Harvard University

I have only an empty list of professional scholars in my family tree, except for mentioning my father and my uncle who failed to become such against a rather strong wish to be one. My father was remembered as a 100 percent professional merchant. But at my good age some old person in town told me that my father had an unusually strong wish for "studying" at his young age. When my father was thirteen years old, his father died and he was forced to succeed in the family business. In protest against his mother's wish, he went on a hunger strike until it was medically pronounced that his life was in danger. Another case was my uncle, who was a student of the Tokyo Institute of Technology. He wished to become a physicist, but because of his father's opposition, he gave up his dream and took an engineering job to support his family. I was lucky to have many brothers, three older and five younger, in addition to six sisters. Indeed I was allowed to enjoy anything abstract: music, math, etc.

Math is simple and clear. I liked that. When my older sister was having math problems, I looked at examples in her textbook, figured out what to do, and then taught her. In my high school days, I once listen to a lecture by a university math professor and I was puzzled by his words, "Mathematics is a mirror of the world." What kind of "mirror" could math be? When I entered Kyoto University, I joined in a seminar group for theoretical physics, but even then I was convinced of my love of mathematics. Later I joined in the seminar group on algebraic geometry organized by Professor Yasuo Akizuki and several active research mathematicians. I was the youngest and the most beloved in the group. I remember I was unusually excited when one member taught me about the work of Oscar Zariski on the problem of resolution of singularities.

Luckily, in 1956, I met Harvard professor Oscar Zariski, who was visiting Kyoto. I was moreover pleased that I could enter Harvard Graduate School. There I learned a great deal not only from Professor Zariski but also from his students such as Michael Artin, David Mumford, Steven Kleiman, and others. It was my luck that I met Alexander Grothendieck at Harvard, who offered me an invitation to the Institut des Hautes Études Scientifiques (IHES), Paris. In 1959, IHES was the smallest mathematical institute among all that I have ever heard of, with only a director, two professors, and one secretary. I was the only visiting fellow. However, the Grothendieck seminar at IHES was a great center of gravity among the mathematical community of Paris.

With a PhD from Harvard in 1960, I got my first job and I married. I had a daughter and a son. At about that time I realized I had everything needed to prove the resolution of singularities in all dimensions. The bits and pieces of technical ideas came together and crystallized into a single proof, based upon what I had acquired earlier: (1) commutative algebra from Kyoto, (2) geometry of polynomials from Harvard, (3) globalization technique from IHES. I call this my Lucky Triplet. I was excited and immediately telephoned Professor Zariski. He responded by saying, "You must have strong teeth," and he proposed starting a seminar. As I began presenting my proof before algebraic geometers from Harvard and MIT, I then realized some logical inadequacy in the definitions I started with. I told Oscar that I needed a recess from the seminar. He agreed. Rewriting the whole paper took me months of concentrated effort. When I met with Oscar on the campus, he kindly asked me, "Is your theorem still a theorem?" and I answered, "Yes, still a theorem." We mathematicians know quite well that a "theorem" (thought to be proven) may go back to being a "conjecture" (yet to be determined true or false). After three months or so, I completed a long paper with a single theorem: Resolution of Singularities.

ERIKO HIRONAKA

Geometric topology

Associate Professor of Mathematics, Florida State University

When I was about twelve years old, I remember my father sitting by a large fireplace in an old farmhouse nestled in the French Alps. He was talking with three of his students. I sat nearby, happily reading a book, enjoying the snow falling outside and the cozy warmth within. Suddenly my father and his younger colleagues stopped talking and were deep in thought. The stillness startled me and seemed to last an eternity, yet they all seemed quite comfortable and absorbed in their world. After a time someone said something and everyone smiled with a quiet pleasure and delight. I thought that whatever mathematics is, it must be beautiful.

Mathematics drew me inexorably, but I also felt uncomfortable devoting myself to a field in which my father was so famous, and did not start studying mathematics until relatively late in college. My ambivalence took time to dissipate, and I alternated between devoting a great deal of energy to my work and to cultivating a life separate from what can seem at times to be a stiflingly small and competitive world. Now, at long last, I have achieved a satisfying balance, with my two young children, a jazz musician husband, and a fulfilling university career.

In retrospect, I realize that I always had a passion for abstract thinking. I was brought up in a bilingual household and went to public schools in places as far apart as Massachusetts, Japan, and France. I learned to love the moments of understanding that can emerge out of the initial chaos and seeming contradictions of a different language and culture. What is "clearly normal" in one place is often "clearly strange" in another: Japanese people eat raw fish but almost never raw carrots; Americans are OK with walking outside barefooted and not removing their shoes when entering a house.

My mathematical research has gravitated toward finding new connections between seemingly distant fields. Over the last several years I've been interested in algebraic integers and surface homeomorphisms. We usually think of numbers as standing alone and static, while surface homeomorphisms generate dynamics. Yet both have well-defined complexity, or distance from the simplest models. Analogous questions can be asked in each context. How does the complexity behave? Given one complex object, is there always another with even smaller complexity? If there are minimally complex objects, what are they like? I have approached these questions using combinatorial constructions that give rise simultaneously to algebraic integers and surface homeomorphisms, revealing hidden relations between them.

As a young child I was amazed at how shapes and patterns can jump out of the sounds of a symphony, or how numbers can seem to have associated colors. From there it does not seem such a stretch to see common features in algebraic integers, low-dimensional algebraic varieties and singularities, complements of knots and links, homeomorphisms of surfaces, and Coxeter systems. I am thankful to be involved in an endeavor that meshes so well with my childhood imaginings. Most of all, I feel fortunate to have been able to experience, in my own way, some of the wonder and enjoyment that I saw in my father and his students as they sat by the fireplace at the farmhouse so many years ago.

JOHN WILLARD MILNOR

Differential topology, K-theory
Fields Medal
Professor of Mathematics and Co-Director of the Institute for Mathematical Sciences, State University of New York, Stony Brook

I first realized that I wanted to be a mathematician during my freshman year at Princeton. I had dabbled in mathematics before—my father was an electrical engineer who owned assorted books on engineering-style mathematics (and also a ridiculously terse primer on complex function theory, translated from German). But in Princeton I discovered that mathematics is much easier than other subjects!

Physics fascinated me, but the courses often seemed boring, with lab experiments that never quite worked. A music course taught me that I have no ear for music; a philosophy course was totally arid; and a creative writing professor read my poem to the class as an example of what to avoid. By way of contrast, I felt immediately at home in the mathematics department. Socially quite backward, I had little idea of how to interact with people. But the mathematics commons room was a joy, with lively conversations and an assortment of games such as chess, Go, and Kriegspiel, watched by interested kibitzers. The international atmosphere, a result of the mass exodus of mathematicians from Nazi Europe, was completely new to me. (We sometimes described the place as the "Department of Broken English.") At Princeton, experts such as Ralph Fox, Norman Steenrod, and Emil Artin taught me the fascination of mathematical ideas and the challenge of mathematical problems.

My most surprising mathematical discovery came almost by accident. Fifty years ago, I was trying to understand the structure of manifolds: smooth objects like the surface of an egg or an inner tube, but in higher dimensions. In 3-dimensional space, if one starts with an object with edges and corners, such as a cube, one can always round off the edges (by the mathematical equivalent of sandpaper) so as to obtain a smooth surface. The surprise was that in higher dimensions, there may be many completely different smoothings. In particular, for the 7-dimensional surface of an 8-dimensional cube, there are twenty-eight essentially different smooth manifolds which can be obtained by carefully chosen smoothings—these are the so-called exotic 7-spheres. I wasn't expecting such a result, or looking for it. Rather, I simply came upon an apparent contradiction when trying to describe possible manifolds in two different ways. The only way to resolve this contradiction was by positing the existence of such exotic spheres, a conclusion which has led to entirely new fields of research.

Of course, such developments never occur in a vacuum. The realm of mathematical ideas has been building at an accelerating pace for more than two thousand years, and my arguments depended heavily on old and new work by mathematicians in England, France, Germany, Switzerland, and the United States.

Outside of mathematics, what I love most is to be in the mountains. Although never an expert, I have very fond memories of climbing and skiing, both in the Alps and in North America, and am always eager to return to high country.

JOAN S. BIRMAN

Topology, knot theory
Professor Emeritus of Mathematics, Barnard College, Columbia University

Why did I choose mathematics? I'm not sure that "choose" is the right word; rather, mathematics chose me. As a very young child I always wanted to understand how things work: figuring out how to build a sturdy windmill that would turn without falling apart, out of rods and spools, was one example. Predicting the swirling patterns made by many rolling marbles was another. I was fascinated by such questions, enjoyed a certain kind of solitary play, and often didn't want to leave it for meals when I was called, much as I don't find it easy to stop working on a math problem today. As soon as I realized that mathematics is filled with thought-provoking questions and gives you tools for their solutions, I was drawn to it. For example, an elementary school teacher asked whether the product of two odd numbers is odd or even. What about an even number and an odd number? Why? Such questions were a challenge, and I responded to the challenge. Equally important was the fact that I did well, and to be good at something reinforces one's natural interest. So in many ways mathematics chose me, although I took many detours before settling on a career in mathematics, because life's big choices are never simple. My particular specialty within math also chose me. When I was faced with deciding on a PhD thesis topic, I did lots of hunting, but the moment I learned about an unanswered question that involved braids, I was hooked! Braids and knots are ubiquitous in nature. There are pictures in my files of braids in Saturn's rings, of long knotted loops of DNA, and even a very clear knot in a picture of the Ebola virus. More important from my viewpoint, braids and knots are also ubiquitous in mathematics.

The study of knots is part of an area of mathematics called topology. Yet here is an example, from my own work, of a way in which knots appeared unexpectedly in a part of mathematics that is far from topology, namely differential equations. In the 1960s the meteorologist E. N. Lorenz became interested in weather prediction. His belief was that weather was governed by a very large system of differential equations, and if so, it should be accurately predictable forever if one knew it at any one moment. Alas, that was far from the case, for while meteorologists know how a hurricane starts, they cannot, even with the most powerful computers, predict its long-time future path or severity with any real accuracy. Aiming for better understanding, Lorenz looked for the simplest example possible of this unpredictability and was led to a system of differential equations in three variables that illustrated the phenomenon, even though they no longer related to weather. The solutions to his equations turned out to be the paradigm for what we know today as "chaos." In my own work with R. F. Williams in the mid 1980s we learned that the closed orbits in the solution to Lorenz's equations are a vast collection of infinitely many different knots; also, any two of these knots cannot be separated without cutting one of them. This requires lots of structure, because all those knots have to fit into a smooth flow in 3-space. Now, knot theory and differential equations are very far-apart areas of mathematics, and nobody was thinking about knotting in this situation. We now understand that, loosely speaking, in any system of differential equations which governs a chaotic flow in a region of 3-space, the number and variety of knots that occur is a measure of just how chaotic the system is. The implications of Lorenz knots, is, as I write, a subject that is still being studied.

FRANCES KIRWAN

Algebraic and symplectic geometry

Professor of Mathematics, University of Oxford

It is one thing to do research in mathematics, and quite another to explain it to nonmathematicians, or even to fellow mathematicians working in different parts of the subject. This is one of the more frustrating aspects of being a research mathematician, although it is at least partially outweighed by the way that mathematics transcends political and cultural boundaries: the authors of the next research paper I pick up to read are as likely to be Indian, Japanese, Russian, or Brazilian as to come from my own country. So instead of trying to describe what my research involves (studying moduli spaces in algebraic geometry), here are some memories of how (I think) I turned into a mathematician.

My earliest mathematical memory is of my father explaining to me the proof of the theorem of Pythagoras on right-angled triangles; it was the first time I had come across the idea that it is possible to prove that something is always true. The next, much later, is of the first lecture I attended as an undergraduate at Cambridge: the lecturer (Tom Körner) took off his shoes and socks and tried to put them on again in the wrong order, to demonstrate to us that composing operations is not in general commutative. I am ashamed to say that this was the only mathematics lecture I went to at Cambridge for which I still have a clear picture of the lecturer and what he (it was always he, not she, with perhaps one exception) was telling us.

Then came the moment when I remember feeling like a research mathematician for the first time. It was at one of the weekly meetings I had as a graduate student at Oxford with my supervisor, Michael Atiyah. At the previous session we had talked about a special case of what would become my PhD topic. Over the intervening week, I had realized that what we had glibly conjectured was not right, and I had worked out how to correct it. When we met again I discovered that my supervisor had thought along exactly the same lines, which was very satisfying.

The satisfaction of a shared understanding of the solution to a difficult problem is one of the main reasons I enjoy collaborating in my research work. The first occasion, more than twenty years ago, was while I was at Harvard as a junior fellow (a postdoctoral position). I gave a seminar at Yale, where Ronnie Lee suggested a collaboration: this led to many discussions, which were both entertaining and educational for me, and eventually to some joint papers. It is also rewarding to work on one's own, but when inspiration dawns, it is usually accompanied by the urge to explain to others the new clarity which it has brought. Collaborators, who have been thinking hard about the same questions, tend to be very happy to listen (and can often point out the flaw in the argument if one exists). Without them, a suitable audience is not always easy to find: I can express my excitement on making some progress to my husband and children, for example, and they will be pleased, but they will certainly not want to hear an explanation of what I have done!

ROBION KIRBY

Low-dimensional topology

Professor of Mathematics, University of California, Berkeley

I was lucky to be born in 1938: I was never in danger of being drafted. I was also lucky to have excellent parents, both educated with a bit of graduate school, but comparatively poor. My father was a (quiet) conscientious objector during World War II and hence lost a few jobs. He then went back to graduate school at age forty-one in 1948, and we lived on a teaching assistant's salary until I went to the University of Chicago in 1954. The lack of money can influence a child in various ways, but in my case it seemed as though I learned that material goods were not so important and not so hard to do without. A fair number of mathematicians are minimalists, as I tend to be.

I grew up in small towns in Washington and Idaho. Knowing arithmetic and how to read before I entered school meant that I was usually bored and spent my time reading or daydreaming in the back of the class. The best school was a three-room school in Farragut, Idaho, where I could do the fifth-grade work as well as my own fourth-grade work and thus skipped a grade. Moreover, I adopted the tendency to not listen to lectures, in fact to teachers or coaches or anyone with whom I was not engaged in a back-and-forth conversation. Games engaged me: chess, poker, and a wide variety of small sports, but not team sports, where one spent too much time listening to a coach or standing in right field.

It became clear, somewhat by elimination, that math was the subject for me. It had always been easy, but I was no prodigy. Around age ten, I had spent hours at school trying to cross the bridges of Königsberg once only, without it ever occurring to me that I might prove that it can't be done. On the other hand, I could beat everyone easily at chess, including my father. Our college team won the US intercollegiate championship twice, and I became ranked twenty-fifth in the country without too much effort. I began to lose interest and sometimes wondered if I could do anything else as well as chess. Eventually I became more interested in math, finally deciding that it was, in fact, the best game of all. This began in my fourth year at Chicago while doing the problems in John Kelley's book, *General Topology*. I'd had a number of friends in law school who often returned from class with some fascinating tort or constitutional law case. I wondered a bit about a law career but decided that for my bread and butter I preferred math.

Ignoring advice to go elsewhere, I snuck into grad school at Chicago, barely passing the exams, and then became really interested in research. As a grad student I had become interested in the annulus conjecture. Saunders Mac Lane advised me that it was a bit hard for a thesis problem (it was), but I thought about it whenever I had an idea. In 1968, while looking after my four-month-old son, an idea occurred to me, now called the "torus trick." It only took a few days to realize that I had reduced the annulus conjecture to a problem about PL homotopy tori, and in a different direction had proved the local contractibility of the space of homeomorphisms of n-space.

I had already arranged to spend fall 1968 at the Institute for Advanced Study, a fortuitous choice because I met Larry Siebenmann, who was the perfect collaborator. We finished off the annulus conjecture and another couple of Milnor's problems, the existence and uniqueness of triangulations of manifolds of dimension greater than four. This used results of Terry Wall, which had been recently proved but not yet entirely written down.

Here again, luck was in my favor. If I had been smarter and seen the torus trick a few years earlier, then I would have reduced these theorems to a problem of non-simply connected surgery, and Wall would have put the last piece of the puzzle in place, thus gaining the final glory. (Adage: prove your theorems at the best time!)

At age thirty, my career was made. (Reality meant that I was not likely to be so lucky again, that my very best work was probably behind me, like many an athlete entering his thirties.) I moved to Berkeley, getting closer to the mountains and rivers that I loved, and adding another fifty PhD students to my mathematical family. These mathematical sons and daughters and further descendants are great friends and one of the best parts of my career.

When I was in high school, much was said about being well-rounded rather than too specialized. But I dismissed this, thinking, "jack of all trades, master of none." Nonetheless, I could not avoid being pulled into other activities. I was a single parent for a number of years with custody of my son and daughter, an avid whitewater kayaker with some classic first descents with Dennis Johnson, a constant thinker about public policy (often with my father and brother), and for twenty-six years now a happy husband of Linda, who enjoys mathematicians more than any other mathematical spouse that I know.

BURT TOTARO

Algebraic geometry, topology, Lie groups
Lowndean Professor of Astronomy and Geometry, University of Cambridge

How did I get started? My mother gives *Sesame Street* a lot of credit, and I think that's fair: I started reading early, because I wanted to know what the words I saw everywhere were saying. My father was a computer programmer in the '60s, when only big companies could afford computers—and the computers themselves were enormous. My father and I played with flowcharts for mathematical problems, and so we were happily ready when the first personal computers appeared in the '70s. At that time, to get a computer to do anything interesting, you really had to program it yourself. That forces you to think hard and systematically, and I found it exciting to think of something I wanted the computer to do and then solve the problem of making it happen.

At school, I liked the stages of increasing sophistication in mathematics. Euclidean geometry is a great step, where you learn how to prove surprising geometric facts starting from simple assumptions. I had some teachers who loved their work, like Florence Kerr and Joe Heiser. Calculus is another tremendous step: mathematics which allows you to describe how things are changing, rather than just a fixed situation.

So up to this point, my story is pretty common. Now, two big pieces of luck come in. First, my parents and I met a psychology professor, Julian Stanley, who was a strong advocate of allowing children to skip grades if they were able to. That worked out well for me. I was ready to start college at thirteen. The second piece of luck is that the university that was willing to take me was the center of American mathematics, Princeton. Besides its mathematics, Princeton's atmosphere was also important. The place is run largely to cater to its undergraduates, so we got a lot of attention, and there was never any danger that I'd get lost in the crowd, which might have happened at a bigger school.

I graduated from Princeton and went to Berkeley as a geometer, but my enthusiasm was already waning a little. I was starting to feel that the subject was too hard for me, and I also wasn't convinced that the very rigid questions involved were really that interesting. Obviously, the two go together: if you aren't interested, you probably don't try hard enough. A particular historical moment at Berkeley came to the rescue. At the time, graduate school at Berkeley was absolutely marinated in topology—famous things like the Jones polynomial for knots were being created. The topology grad students would ask me weird questions about geometric structures, questions a geometer would by training "know" not to ask. Once I accepted the weirdness, it became natural to start thinking about the topology of the geometric shapes I was studying.

Ever since, I have studied geometry from a topological point of view. That means that we take precisely defined shapes, such as circles, but then imagine them to be made of something soft, for example, rubber or string, and stretch them. A lot of different shapes become equivalent from this point of view: you can turn a coffee cup into a doughnut. But some information is still left: you can never turn a ball into a doughnut just by stretching, because of the hole in the doughnut.

In the past, mathematicians always tried to solve problems exactly. Now we realize that most problems will never have an exact solution. Nonetheless, we can hope to understand the general shape of a solution, and topology gives a language for talking about these shapes. Topology gives a new point of view on all kinds of physical phenomena: the collapse of a bridge that vibrates too much, the tangling of strands of DNA, and so on. But I have to admit that my own interest is based on the joy of understanding shapes rather than on any particular applications.

SIMON DONALDSON

Differential geometry, algebraic geometry
Fields Medal
Royal Society Research Professor, Imperial College London

My father had a large influence on my development into a mathematician, at least in a general way. I have an early memory of him saying with relish : ". . . and then I shall be able to get back to research" (presumably, after completing some chores which he had described to me). I had no idea what "research" might be, but from that time the word was tinged with glamour and romance.

My father was an engineer (my two brothers followed him) and was often sceptical of overly theoretical work. "All they produce is paper"—I hear him fulminating—"I bet they haven't touched a screwdriver in years". (Although this was not meant completely seriously; he had a deep interest in all kinds of science). Our house was always full of projects of a creative, practical kind: building model aircraft and so on. My own attempts in this direction were usually less successful; my vision of what I wanted to achieve outran my patience and ability to bring it about. So that was partly how I moved towards mathematics, where vision was not trammeled by irksome practical difficulties. Another thing that was very important was that I was fascinated by sailing, sailing boats, and anything nautical. So, when I was about thirteen, I decided that my career was to be a yacht designer, and began to design some. (I had no intention of actually building these yachts—that could wait until I had wealthy clients—so the enterprise was not limited by practicalities.) I went into this deeply. To design a yacht you need to calculate volumes, areas, moments, and so on from your plans. So it was quite natural for me to learn more mathematics. Gradually, the mathematics became the center of my interests and the yacht designing fell into the background.

I was also lucky to have excellent mathematics teachers. It was important for me to be able to do well in mathematics and physics at school. A large influence in that direction came from my grandfather. He was a teacher of modern languages and, at a younger age, encouraged my interest in history and academic things generally.

By the time I was about sixteen, I had a fairly definite idea that what I wanted to be was a mathematician and some notion of what that was. I would investigate various questions that occurred to me, almost never making any definite progress. So in a way I was precocious (although definitely not in the sense of being particularly good at tests of the Mathematical Olympiad kind or, later, the undergraduate exams in Cambridge). This made the transition to life as a proper research mathematician, as a doctoral student in Oxford with Nigel Hitchin and Michael Atiyah, comparatively easy for me.

I mostly work by drawing pictures (vestiges of my yacht plans?) so I was naturally attracted to geometry. When I was an undergraduate, it was not so easy to learn about differential geometry, since it did not really come into the standard course, but this added to the allure of the subject. Holding fast to my metaphorical paternal screwdriver, I prefer problems that are quite concrete and specific, where one feels one is actually producing and working with some definite mathematical object.

I was blessed with good fortune at the start of my research career. At that time (1980) the Yang–Mills equations, arising in particle physics, were making a big impact in pure mathematics, particularly in connection with geometry and Roger Penrose's twistor theory. The project Hitchin suggested to me involved a rather different kind of question, connecting differential and algebraic geometry but veering more towards analysis and partial differential equations. Happily—with rather different purposes in mind, Karen Uhlenbeck and Cliff Taubes had, in the few years before, gone a long way in developing the relevant analytical techniques. Of course this was before the Internet made it so easy to find papers, and I remember the exciting day when I received Uhlenbeck's preprints by mail from the USA. This was when I was a first-year doctoral student. A good approach in research, I find, is to imagine what should be true, i.e., a picture of what properties some mathematical objects have, and then explore the consequences. If the consequences lead to a contradiction, that shows that the picture needs to be modified; on the other hand, if the consequences fit in with what one knows otherwise and lead to some interesting further predictions, that is good evidence for the correctness of the picture. Following this strategy (although certainly not consciously) and exploring the properties of Yang–Mills instantons, I stumbled on, at the beginning of my second year, an entirely unexpected application of these to the topology of four-dimensional manifolds. The two main themes of my research in the twenty-seven years since then have been extending this and, in a different direction, developing the links between algebraic geometry, differential geometry, and partial differential equations.

HENRI CARTAN

Algebraic topology, complex analysis

Professor Emeritus of Mathematics, University of Paris-Sud Orsay

I learned to read at home. My family lived in Paris and at six, I was sent to the Lycée Buffon. After the first test paper, I told my parents I was very proud because I came in twenty-fourth. To me this high number was a proof of excellence. It was explained that it was better to be first, which I managed to be from then on.

We spent the summer in a little village in Isère, Dolomieu, near the family smithy where my father, Élie Cartan, had spent his youth. His extraordinary gift for mathematics had been detected by his schoolmaster, and he brilliantly worked his way to the Académie des Sciences. He was a very modest man. He was probably conscious of his personal worth but never flaunted it. He did not talk me into doing mathematics, but I was always welcome to converse with him and ask him questions. I remember one day when we were walking in the woods, he told me that Euclid's postulate was not a necessity. I found it very hard to swallow! Much later we worked on a few problems together, but usually we worked on our own.

I knew from the beginning I would specialize in mathematics. To me it was the fundamental science par excellence. When I got my baccalauréat, it was quite clear to me that I would take the competitive entrance exam for the École Normale Supérieure in mathematics. Yet many things bothered me about the math I was taught. I remember that the beginnings of geometry were disconcerting to me. Unconsciously, I felt the axioms were not stated in a satisfactory way. So when I started teaching, I made sure that everything was logically coherent. I was soon reputed to be a finicky perfectionist!

I turned to my friend André Weil for advice. We were both teaching in the same university in Strasbourg. I must say that I certainly tried his patience with my questions. He decided we would meet in Paris with a few other mathematicians to work on a treatise of mathematical analysis. He would then be freed from my constant questioning. This is how the Bourbaki group began.

Our venture soon proved to be gigantic. We had to start from the basis of mathematics all over again. I loved the challenge and I was only too glad to work alongside so many good friends. In fact, most of the mathematics I learned was through Bourbaki during our joint research work. I greatly enjoyed discovering what was true and demonstrating it as simply and elegantly as possible. I also devoted much of my time to teaching mathematics, being very eager to make my students share my passion. I felt strongly that I belonged to a new generation of scientists who had to radically change the way certain mathematical theories were presented.

Beside mathematics, I am very keen on music. One of my brothers, Jean, was a very gifted composer who died early of tuberculosis. Music has always been—and still is—part and parcel of my daily life. So is politics. At the end of World War II, I was very grateful to some of my German colleagues for attempting to find news of my other brother, Louis, who had been sent to a concentration camp for belonging to the Resistance and was put to death there. I then realized that friendship between men is something that can exist independently of jingoistic prejudices. As a result of this experience, I was inspired to assume responsibilities, particularly in the liberation of Soviet dissidents. Since 1952, I have militated actively in favor of a federal Europe, free from the logic of national interests. Now that I am in the evening of my life, I still hope my dream will come true.

ROBERT D. MACPHERSON

Differential geometry, algebraic geometry

Hermann Weyl Professor of Mathematics, Institute for Advanced Study, Princeton

My father, a physicist, used the word "mathematician" exclusively as a put-down. A "mathematician" was someone with no physical intuition who was caught up in irrelevant problems. He finally saw an upside to my choice of a career when he realized that as a byproduct of doing mathematics, I got to experience different cultures. The mathematical community is really international. A proof is a proof, no matter what language it is in. Furthermore, mathematicians do not have laboratories, so we can move around. I have lived in ten countries for at least a month, and I have mathematical friends from many more.

My choice of career was not so obvious at first. In college, I spent more time on physics and music than on mathematics. In the end, I went into mathematics because mathematicians seemed to genuinely appreciate and to respect each other's work. I still find this to be true, and it makes the atmosphere among professional mathematicians more pleasant than what I know of other subjects. The downside to mathematics as a career is that, when an idea doesn't work, you usually have nothing at all. No charisma or erudition can redeem a wrong proof.

I have always preferred working in unpopular areas of mathematics. I recognize the benefits of working in popular areas—a community of experts to discuss problems with, a group of friends you see regularly at conferences, a reference group to compare yourself to, a crowd to instantly appreciate your newest results—but it's not for me.

However, even if you're working in an unpopular area, when you find some fertile ideas, people will notice and pile into your area. My solution is to get out and move to another area that is less crowded.

I am a geometer at heart. When I discover a mathematical idea, it comes as a geometric mental picture that completely convinces me. It is always a real struggle to translate my mental picture into words so that I can communicate it. Once I have put it into words, it seems much less vivid and real to me than my original mental image did. I have lived during a time when most of the world's true geometers have worked in low-dimensional topology, a subject that, however beautiful, has never tempted me personally. I have worked in areas dominated by algebraists, who generally have very little difficulty translating their thoughts into words. In my view, significant mathematical progress requires contributions from a variety of approaches. To make a useful contribution to mathematics, it is less important to be brilliant than to have a unique and original approach.

Nearly all my mathematical papers are joint work. I dislike working alone. Working jointly compensates for my lack of facility with words. It also addresses the problem of the basic loneliness of mathematical research. My best work has been done jointly with Mark Goresky. We spent years working on the homology of singular spaces at a time when very few other mathematicians cared about it. We have since moved on to other mathematical projects as mathematical partners, and he has become my life partner as well.

MICHAEL FREEDMAN

Topology, physics, computer science
Fields Medal
Director, Station Q, Microsoft and University of California, Santa Barbara

My father, Benedict, was a child prodigy in mathematics, musical, and also a brilliant writer. I had already regressed toward the mean. Still, as a child, I also displayed certain peculiar mathematical talents but was not exceptionally strong in computation. Outside of mathematics, I had no other demonstrable talents. However, I painted in an expressionist style and this, my mother, Nancy, convinced me, showed genius. I learned quite young that mathematics also was an art form and felt certain I could make a mark upon it. This certainty was based really on nothing but exuberant overconfidence, to which I can credit only my mother's absolute faith in my abilities. It did not, in that day, seem to be necessary to provide any supporting evidence to the claim of mathematical precocity. I was accepted at all my schools from elementary to graduate as a prodigy. I took few tests and do not remember doing extremely well on any. These days, I often meet actual prodigies—typically their mothers bring them to me—and feel a bit embarrassed that I once thought I was one.

At sixteen I had not yet chosen between mathematics and painting. I went to UC Berkeley as a freshman with all my clothes, towels, sheets, and blanket used to pad my paintings within two large suitcases. My mother told me to show the paintings to the chairman of the art department and to see what happened. It was a Friday afternoon when I arrived and the chairman was out. I ended up leaving the suitcases with his secretary to be locked in his office, having forgotten they also contained my clothes. That night I was alone in the apartment I would eventually be sharing. I had no bedding or extra clothes and could not get the heat on. I found I could stay warm and asleep in the bathtub for about one hour at a time before having to recharge with fresh hot water. I don't remember the exact process, but I soon decided on math.

Near the end of my first year at Berkeley I was playing Go with an astronomy postdoc who had just arrived from Princeton. I was lamenting that I could not understand any of the French in language lab. All the words seemed run together and I despaired of sorting them out. I was starting to get language-lab nightmares. He knew a champion Go player, Ralph Fox, in the math department at Princeton. I worked up a two-pronged plan to apply immediately to graduate school at Princeton and temporarily solve my problem with French. I read Fox's book on knot theory and included my own conjecture on what I considered a bold generalization of his subject: to "links," knots with several pieces. What I conjectured was wrong but apparently that was not considered decisive. (Basically I conjectured that nothing like the three-ring logo on a can of Ballantine Ale could exist—well I was only seventeen and did not drink beer yet.) As a second army for this great pincer maneuver, my father helped me flush out my thoughts on "modal logic," and into the application they went. But the decisive ingredient turned out to be my mother's insistence on including a large photo of her son taken as I teetered on the tip of a granite spire on North Palisade.

Many years later I learned from Ed Nelson (a professor at Princeton) that he was in the office with Fox when my late-arriving application was brought in. According to Ed, when Ralph tore open the envelope, the picture fluttered to the floor. Ralph picked it up and said, "Let's admit this one." I had told my mother that it was completely inappropriate to include a picture and that they would make their decision on scholarly factors. She had been an actress and told me, "Everything is show business." On this occasion she was right.

That got me started. I may have had one or two other close calls but there was no turning back. I've been thinking about mathematics and physics for forty years and have found certainty and surprise, universality and unicity. Quantum mechanics changes one's view of the world. It shows the world to be so miraculous that it is difficult to worry.

DUSA MCDUFF

von Neumann algebras, symplectic geometry

Helen Lyttle Kimmel Professor of Mathematics, Barnard College, Columbia University

Born in London just after the Second World War, I grew up in Edinburgh. My father was an embryologist and geneticist, interested in how organisms develop but also deeply interested in art, philosophy, and the uses of science. My mother was an architect, who worked in the town-planning department of the Scottish Civil Service. She always had a job, which was unusual for the time, and brought me up to think that I would also have a career. Her father had read mathematics at Cambridge University and then became a distinguished lawyer; my talent in mathematics came from that side of the family. Architecture, after all, combines mathematics with design.

My grandfather taught me the multiplication tables when I was four. He had me on his knee and showed me a table of all the multiplications up to 10 times 10, pointing out the symmetries. I still remember how beautiful I found it. I always loved doing sums at school. Later, I grew interested in music, poetry, and philosophy but always took for granted that I would have an academic career. When I was a teenager and wondering what on earth I should do, I realized that mathematics was what I loved; it spoke to me somehow. I saw mathematics as comparable to abstract painting. I didn't know any female mathematicians, but I didn't mind. I wanted to be different.

In Cambridge for my PhD, I solved a problem that had been open for twenty years. There was a certain algebraic structure that people had defined and studied, but they neither had many examples nor knew how many different objects of this kind could exist. I constructed infinitely many different ones. My thesis was published in the *Annals of Mathematics*, arguably the leading mathematics journal, and for a long time it was my best work.

After I wrote my thesis, I went to Moscow where in the late '60s they had an absolutely marvelous school of mathematics. It was very broad and open, a real contrast to the narrow education I had had up until then. I worked with Israel Gelfand for six months, a transforming experience. Upon my return, I completely changed my focus from functional analysis to topology. However, I was now so aware of my ignorance that it was very hard to become creative in the new field. I only survived as a mathematician because of the confidence my thesis gave me. I moved to the United States in the late '70s and have worked here ever since. Now I work in symplectic geometry, studying a particular kind of structure on space that mathematicians formulated in the nineteenth century while investigating questions in physics.

I once tried to explain my PhD work to my mother. It was an interesting conversation: she really wanted to know what I was doing and she was certainly very intelligent. However, I realized that the number of new concepts that I had to tell her, made it completely impossible to explain what the objects that I was thinking about really were. To get anywhere, mathematicians have to internalize the ideas they use. Mathematical objects do not just satisfy a list of axioms; they have feeling, shape, texture, and move around in a particular way in the mind. We have to learn to manipulate them, understand how they interrelate. This takes time and effort. Understanding, when it comes, is often nonverbal, a flashing realization that this is how things fit together.

WILLIAM PAUL THURSTON

Topology
Fields Medal
Professor of Mathematics, Cornell University

"To understand" was the goal I gave for my high school yearbook, and this is still what drives me. I love to reach understanding: first, to see something (big or little) that doesn't make sense or is simply discordant, then to reflect and ponder, to search and stare in my mind's eye until sometimes, miraculously, vision is transformed and mist and muddle develop into form, order, and connection.

Mathematics is not about numbers, equations, computations, or algorithms: it is about understanding. I've loved mathematics all my life, although I often doubted that mathematics would turn out to be my life's focus even when others thought it obvious. I hated much of what was taught as mathematics in my early schooling, and I often received poor grades. I now view many of these early lessons as anti-math: they actively tried to discourage independent thought. One was supposed to follow an established pattern with mechanical precision, put answers inside boxes, and "show your work," that is, reject mental insights and alternative approaches. My attention is more inward than that of most people: it can be resistant to being captured and directed externally. Exercises like these mathematics lessons were excruciatingly boring and painful (whether or not I had "mastered the material"). I used to think my wandering attention and difficulty in completing assignments was a defect, but I now realize my "laziness" is a feature, not a bug. Human society wouldn't function well if everyone were like me, but society is better with everyone not being alike.

I went to a small college in the year (1964) that it started; New College in Sarasota, Florida, drawn by their discussion of educational philosophy in comparison to all the other college catalogues that I studied. This was a formative experience. There was a strong emphasis on the idea that students ultimately are responsible for their own education, there was a vision of a community of scholars including students and faculty, and there was a strong component of independent study: the initial schedule was three month-long independent study projects every year. I took these very seriously. I was very curious and ambitious to dig into the things that were mysteries. My first independent study project was titled "Language," and the second "Thought."

Whether in spite of or because of their naively ambitious scope, I got a lot out of these projects, and what I learned then has significantly woven into how I work.

Mathematics has been a fantastic experience for me. I found a community of people with whom I felt comfortable. I was awed by the amazingly intricate and beautiful edifices that could be built from simple rules by pure thought. I have savored sweeping transformations continually taking place in our vision and understanding of mathematical subjects.

The biggest strand in my own work is three-dimensional geometry and topology. Imagine you are in a large cubical room, and now imagine that the front wall is identified with the back wall: in other words, when you look straight forward, your line of sight continues, jumping from the front wall to the back, and you see the back of your head. Your lines of sight continue, so what you see is images of everything in the room, repeated forward and backward as far as the eye can see. Now imagine that the left wall is identified with the right wall, and the floor is identified with the ceiling. Your lines of sight repeat in all directions, and you will see images of yourself and whatever else is in the room arrayed in a three-dimensional repeating pattern, as in the structure of a crystal. This construction yields one possible three-dimensional world (or universe), known as the 3-torus. There are many other possible topologies for a three-dimensional world. A huge variety of examples can be constructed by starting with other polyhedra, not just the cube, and identifying pairs of faces.

When I began my career, it was assumed that these three-dimensional worlds were typically hopelessly shapeless, but I gradually came to the realization that three-dimensional worlds typically come from beautiful geometrically repeating patterns, not usually in ordinary (Euclidean) space, but in one of eight kinds of three-dimensional geometries: the vast majority actually are in hyperbolic space. I formulated a conjecture, known as the "geometrization conjecture," making this precise, and I proved it in many cases. This conjecture (which includes the famous Poincaré conjecture) has now been proven by Grigori Perelman.

BERTRAM KOSTANT

Lie groups, differential geometry, mathematical physics
Professor Emeritus of Mathematics, Massachusetts Institute of Technology

I was in high school during the Second World War, and although I was good in mathematics, my main scientific interest was in chemistry. However, I was very undisciplined with regard to homework and I did badly in nonscience subjects. Consequently I was rejected from admission to first-rank universities.

Nevertheless, things turned out very well indeed. The theme of what I now want to say is that by some quirk of fate I seemed to be at the right place at the right time. In the postwar period, German academic refugees brought an infusion of European science to American universities. Purdue University, where I was accepted, had a number of excellent mathematicians on its faculty. One such person was Arthur Rosenthal, who had been chairman of the Department of Mathematics in Munich around 1920. One of his students there was Werner Heisenberg, and one of his close colleagues was the man who finally proved that the circle cannot be squared, Ferdinand Lindemann. I became very friendly with Rosenthal, and it was he more than anyone else who influenced me to devote myself to mathematical research.

Another piece of good luck was that the dean of science at Purdue was a mathematician, William Ayres, who gave me special permission, even though I was an undergraduate, to take three excellent graduate courses. I did well enough to win a graduate fellowship to the University of Chicago. Here was another piece of good luck. Chicago in the early 1950s was intellectually an extremely exciting place. These were the last years of the presidency of Robert Hutchins. The faculty, recruited by the chairman of the mathematics department, Marshall Stone, included such stars as André Weil, S. S. Chern, and Saunders Mac Lane.

In one of my courses, a lifelong love affair with Lie groups began for me as soon as I opened Claude Chevalley's then relatively recent book on this subject. Lie group theory serves to unify diverse areas of mathematics. Pursuing such unifications has been the focus of much of my subsequent mathematical research activities. Chevalley was French, and in general, I was very much attracted to the French school of mathematics, especially the mathematics of Bourbaki.

My doctoral thesis adviser (I. E. Segal) arranged for me to spend 1954–1956 at Princeton's Institute for Advanced Study. The timing for this was yet another fortunate coincidence. Among the institute's members were three of the most outstanding contributors to twentieth-century science: Hermann Weyl, John von Neumann, and Albert Einstein. By 1956, when I left Princeton, all three had died. While at the institute I became very friendly with Weyl and had mathematical discussions with von Neumann. I had only one long memorable conversation with Einstein. It was on Good Friday in 1955. At one point Einstein asked me what I was working on. I replied Lie groups, thinking, however, that he probably didn't know who Lie was. I was pleasantly surprised when he countered with the prescient remark, "That will be very important." About a week later Einstein was dead.

In 1957, I joined the mathematics department at UC Berkeley. This was a period of tremendous growth at Berkeley and I was happy to be a part of it. In 1962 I accepted an offer of full professorship at MIT. At MIT opportunities presented themselves to build a world famous center for Lie groups and related subjects.

Complicated objects can often be studied by first dealing with their symmetries. Lie groups are mathematical structures designed to study and deal with different kinds of symmetry. Many of these structures are very sophisticated and one can spend a lifetime exploring their intricacies. Results about one such Lie group, called E_8, attracted considerable media attention recently mainly because a team of approximately twenty five mathematicians, using a vast computer program, determined the enormous list of its "characters." In my opinion, E_8 is the most magnificent "object" in all of mathematics. E_8 is like a diamond with thousands of facets where each facet offers a beautiful different view of its internal structure. It is mysterious that the laws of nature are eventually written in mathematical terms. Attempts have been made to involve E_8 in our understanding of elementary particles. Judging from criticisms, it is likely that these first attempts are flawed. Still, one cannot help having the gut feeling that a real understanding of our universe must somehow involve E_8. Many physical theories over the past century seem to have had a shelf life of a few decades. But E_8 is forever!

JOHN N. MATHER

Differential geometry, Hamiltonian dynamics
Professor of Mathematics, Princeton University

I remember being fascinated by logarithms when I was six years old. My father must have explained them to me. He was a professor of electrical engineering at Princeton. From time to time, he liked to teach me some aspects of elementary mathematics.

When I was eleven or so, I found one of my father's engineering textbooks on a shelf at home and I spent a considerable amount of time delving into it. It was basically a calculus text, including the calculus of variations, motivated by lots of applications to engineering problems. There was a lot that I did not understand. I am sure that I could not have passed an exam on the subject of the book. Nonetheless, I found it very interesting, perhaps the more so because I did not understand it very well. I found the fact that one could solve "real life" problems (such as finding the shape of the cable of a suspension bridge) by simple paper-and-pencil calculations very appealing.

My interest in mathematics led me to buy various math books from Dover Publications and the Princeton University bookstore when I was in high school. I bought and delved into Solomon Lefschetz's *Topology*, the first volume of Claude Chevalley's *Lie Groups*, books on group theory by R. D. Carmichael and William Burnside, an English translation of a three-volume *Cours d'Analyse* by Edouard Goursat, and Paul Halmos's *Finite Dimensional Vector Spaces*. I remember spending a great deal of time with all of these books because they fascinated me. On the other hand, with the exception of Halmos's book, which I studied thoroughly, what I understood was only a fraction of what these authors had to say.

In my last semester in high school, I was fortunate to be able to take part in a program initiated by Professor Albert Tucker of the Princeton mathematics department. This enabled bright high school students to take math classes at Princeton University. I was the first to do so. After a brief oral examination, I was placed in a junior-level course in abstract algebra, taught by Ralph Fox. I did perfect work in the course.

I took my undergraduate degree at Harvard University and my graduate degree at Princeton University. When I was in my first year at Princeton, I read notes by Harold Levine of lectures by René Thom on singularities of mappings. I soon solved several open problems described in the notes. My solutions of these problems appeared in a series of six papers on smooth stability of mappings. After completing my degree at Princeton, I spent two years at René Thom's institute, Institut des Hautes Études Scientifiques (IHES) in France. Thom was very accessible and I was very glad that I got to know him. Thom thought he had proved the density of topologically stable mappings, but he had not convinced other mathematicians. I found a modification of his method that mathematicians accepted as a proof. This proof relied mostly on ideas of Thom but also used one significant innovation of mine.

I spent the next four years at Harvard. When I was there, I worked mostly on the theory of foliations and André Haefliger's classifying space. Bill Thurston found a brilliant generalization of my results, leading to the Mather–Thurston theorem, which reduces the study of the topology of Haefliger's classifying space to questions in the homology of groups of diffeomorphisms, most of which, however, remain open.

After four years at Harvard, I decided that I liked Princeton better. I have been at Princeton ever since.

One day, I heard Ian Percival speak at Princeton. He introduced an unusual sort of Lagrangian in his talk. A couple of years later, I made a serendipitous discovery that his Lagrangian could be used to prove an existence theorem. (A similar theorem was proved independently by S. Aubry and P. Y. Le Daeron.) This existence theorem proved to be of considerable interest to experts in Hamilton dynamics, and I have been working in related topics ever since.

MARYAM MIRZAKHANI

Ergodic theory, Teichmüller theory

Professor of Mathematics, Princeton University

I grew up in Iran and had a happy childhood. There were no scientists in my family, but I learned a lot from my older brother, who was always interested in math and science. Around me, women were encouraged to be independent and pursue their interests. I remember watching programs on TV about notable, strong women like Marie Curie and Helen Keller. I admired people who were passionate about their work, and I was impressed with books like *Lust for Life*, about Vincent Van Gogh. However, as a child I dreamt of becoming a writer, and reading novels was my favorite pastime.

Later I got involved in math competitions and became more and more interested in doing mathematics. I had very good friends who were also interested in mathematics, which made my undergraduate years very exciting and inspiring. I majored in math and then went to Harvard as a graduate student. Working with Curt McMullen at Harvard, I became interested in different areas of mathematics related to dynamics and geometry of Riemann surfaces. His broad interest and deep insight had a great influence on me.

Math departments tend to be very much male-dominated and sometimes intimidating for young women. Having said that, however, I have never encountered any issue because I am a woman, and I have had supportive colleagues. Nonetheless, the situation is far from ideal. I believe women are able to do the same work as men, but the timing can be different. It might be easier for men to concentrate for longer periods of time and sacrifice more for their work. Also, what society expects from women is sometimes different from what research requires. It is very important to stay confident and motivated.

I have worked mostly on problems related to the geometry of surfaces and dabbled in related areas. Complex analysis and ergodic theory always fascinated me.

I enjoy learning different areas of mathematics and understanding the connections between them. The wonderful aspect of the problems about Riemann surfaces is the connection with so many fields in mathematics, including ergodic theory, algebraic geometry and hyperbolic geometry.

I am very slow in doing research. I don't believe in boundaries between different areas of mathematics. I like to think about challenging problems that I am excited about, and follow wherever they lead me. This allows me to interact and learn from many smart colleagues. In a way, doing mathematics feels like writing a novel where your problem evolves like a live character. However, you have to be very precise in what you say: everything must fit together like the gears in a clock.

CURTIS MCMULLEN

Complex analysis, topology, geometry and dynamics
Fields Medal
Cabot Professor of Mathematics, Harvard University

In Ohio on July 20, 1969, I somehow got the shutter to stick open on the plastic Kodak camera my parents had brought back from the New York World's Fair. Later that night, we watched Neil Armstrong, also from Ohio, set foot on the moon. When the film was developed, the timed exposure showed the moon as a white comet arcing across the evening sky. Shortly thereafter we moved to the small town of Charlotte, Vermont. In the moving boxes, I found a copy of Daniel McCracken's *Guide to Fortran IV Programming*. Using it and a teletype at the local high school, which was hooked up by phone to the mainframe at the University, I was able to slowly churn out generation after generation of John Conway's Game of Life.

Later, during graduate school, David Mumford introduced me to the rococo limit sets of Kleinian groups, which he was drawing by computer. Dennis Sullivan, at Institut des Hautes Études Scientifiques and the City University of New York, became my thesis advisor. Those years in Paris and New York, learning conformal dynamics with Sullivan's entourage, were the beginning of my professional education.

My mathematical education continued at Princeton. As a postdoc I thought off and on about Kra's conjecture, $\|\Theta\|_{H/X} < 1$; one day I realized it had to be true, because every pyramid scheme contains the seeds of its own collapse. This observation led to a new analytic proof of Thurston's uniformization theorem for 3-manifolds. My work still lies in this field: the crossroads of low-dimensional topology, Riemann surfaces, dynamics, and hyperbolic geometry, where rigidity leads inexorably from the infinities of analysis to the concreteness of arithmetic and algebra. Let me end with an example.

Pictured below is an infinitely complex lacework dividing a sphere into shaded tiles. Underlying the image is a dynamical system given by a simple algebraic formula; each point evolves in one of ten different ways, corresponding to the ten different shades in the picture.

Every motif is replicated endlessly, at smaller and smaller scales. A photograph of a paramecium or the image of a virus from a scanning electron microscope carries a similar hint of infinity: it makes visible a level of structure that is constantly before us, and part of us, but invisibly small. This spherical mosaic has the same symmetries as a classical solid, the dodecahedron; for me, it brings to mind Henri Poincaré and Felix Klein and even Évariste Galois's death in a duel in 1832, shortly after he found a remarkable connection between such symmetries and the unsolvability of quintic polynomials (like $x^5 + 3x + 1 = 0$).

Working at Princeton in 1988, Peter Doyle and I realized that by choosing a point on the sphere at random, we could break the symmetry of the quintic equation and, updating Galois, give a dynamical formula for its solution. The picture below emerged, like a celestial body long orbiting in the void but previously unseen.

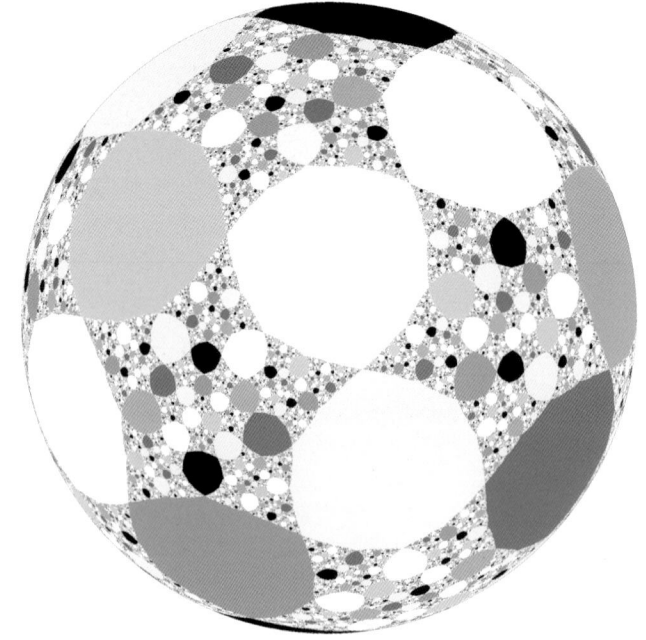

DENNIS PARNELL SULLIVAN

Topology, dynamical systems, geometry, analysis, fluid dynamics, quantum algebra
Einstein Professor of Science, City University of New York Graduate Center,
and Distinguished Professor of Mathematics, State University of New York, Stony Brook

A feature of abstract mathematics that must be surprising to the thoughtful layperson is that in mathematics the concept of infinity can be formally defined and that mathematicians can work with it. Actually mathematics is very special in that each of its concepts can be precisely defined and that this in fact must be so before mathematicians can get to work. Progress in mathematics often depends on the new concepts that are actually created by these new and precise definitions. The combinatorial patterns, geometric pictures, and algebraic calculation that are present in many branches of science are the nourishment for this benevolent monster of precision that guards the realm of abstract mathematics.

Mathematicians derive much comfort from this possibility of complete precision. There is one fly in the ointment, however. The famous theorem of Kurt Gödel states that any logical system containing at least one infinite collection of objects as well as the other basic operations used by mathematicians cannot be proven to be self-consistent. Mathematicians work with the belief that the commonly used logical system with the existence of one infinite collection assumed is actually self-consistent, even if this can never be proved.

The chapter and verse of mathematics is built up from two basic intuitions: the idea of space and the idea of number. Numbers can be built using the existence and the definition of an infinite collection: there is a way to rearrange the collection of elements inside itself which does not cover the entire collection but also does not rearrange two distinct elements of the collection to lie on the same element. Mathematicians call such a rearrangement "a function from the collection to itself which is one-to-one but not onto." One may then consider the smallest collection closed under composition of such functions of the infinite collection into itself that includes the small collection. This constructs entities that play the role of the positive integers. To build space, one then builds from these integers more general numbers and then the number line. Finally, one forms tuples (otherwise called "Cartesian products") to build manifolds, geometries, continuous symmetry groups, calculus and all the modern concepts of present-day mathematics. These concepts have been extremely useful outside the joyful activities of mathematicians to describe physical processes using the theories of Isaac Newton, James Maxwell, Albert Einstein, Ludwig Boltzmann, Werner Heisenberg, and many others.

Recently the combinatorial patterns, geometries, and algebraic calculation that could feed the precision monster of mathematicians have multiplied apace because of quantum field theory and string theory. The process of finding new concepts that would enable the feast or mathematization of these new discoveries is ongoing but far from complete. There are interesting and new algebraic concepts that seem very relevant, that is, the number aspect is going well. However, the fundamental paradigm of space for the feast seems to be missing and much effort has been spent on this problem.

My own proposal, tried as well by others, is that an appropriate model of space suitable for quantum discussions may be based on the idea of breaking usual space into small chambers, which may be further divided but only finitely. Then the algebraic ideas corresponding to approximate identities with an infinite hierarchy of corrections may be spread over this chambering of space using the basic methodology of combinatorial and algebraic topology.

String theory discussions in this philosophy would yield to related differential algebra or differential category discussions. These discussions would treat what remains after applying the least-action principle in infinite dimensional functional spaces that are themselves treated by algebraic topology.

When all of these algebraic patterns are assimilated, the chambering can be allowed to become infinitely small. Then classical limits should be derived based on inequalities and the hard estimates of mathematical analysis. My additional hope is that useful mathematical models of fluid motion in three dimensions can also be developed using these same ideas.

Sometimes I feel like mathematics is still at the beginning; but even failing to solve an interesting intellectual and mathematical problem can be a lot of fun.

STEPHEN SMALE

Topology, dynamical systems
Fields Medal
Professor Emeritus of Mathematics, University of California, Berkeley, and Professor, Toyota Tecnhological Institute at Chicago

I was brought up in a rural area in Michigan. From the age of five to fifteen, I lived on a ten-acre farm. My father worked in the city in the automobile plants. I went to a one-room schoolhouse for eight years, walking more than a mile each way. With one-room schoolhouses, you don't have too many expectations. While I was in high school, my father bought me a small chemical lab and I became obsessed with organic chemistry, even to the extent of foolishly offering to make rare chemicals needed in private industry. I turned to physics when I went to college in Ann Arbor. I failed the physics course, so in my last year of college, I changed to math.

My work was erratic in mathematics graduate school, yet I finished well enough in 1956, largely due to the inspiration of my teacher Raoul Bott. I continued working in topology until the summer of 1961, at which time I declared that I was leaving topology for the more exciting frontier of dynamical systems, then called "the qualitative theory of ordinary differential equations" (I fear that some of my colleagues never forgave me!).

Perhaps my career as a mathematician has had an uncharacteristic number of twists and turns throughout my many years. My fields of research have varied substantially. For example, I have worked in economic equilibrium theory and in complexity theory of computer science. Now my attentions are devoted to learning theory and vision. My work in vision is oriented towards a mathematical model of aspects of the visual cortex as well as what is called pattern recognition. The mathematics is hoped to give some new understanding of the development of neurons in vision and their functioning—in other words, how people see.

Through these years there has been a common theme in the way I think in science. On one hand I am an unabashed theorist. On the other hand the theory is tied to reality using the world of mathematics. Especially during the last four decades, I have devoted myself to the world of human experience. My work is motivated by what other scientists have learned to be important, and by my belief that these areas can be better understood through mathematics. Thus one is led to mathematical foundations for several disciplines in science. My goal is to understand the world better through mathematics. I am inspired in this endeavor by the great mathematical scientists of the past like Isaac Newton in mechanics and John von Neumann and Hermann Weyl in the foundations of quantum mechanics.

In recent decades I have followed another obsession, the collection and photography of natural crystallized mineral specimens. My last book is devoted to this endeavor. Maybe there is a relation between the beauty of mathematics and the beauty of minerals?

MARINA RATNER

Ergodic theory
Professor of Mathematics, University of California, Berkeley

I was born and grew up in Moscow. I fell in love with math when I was in the fifth grade. Traditionally the level of education in the big cities in Russia was very high. The school program in math was rigorous and stimulating. I was fascinated with mathematical reasoning in algebra and geometry, which was beautiful and exciting. Math came naturally to me and I felt unmatched satisfaction solving difficult problems.

There were no mathematicians in my family. My father was a well-known plant physiologist and my mother was a chemist. In the late '40s my mother was fired from her job for corresponding with her mother in Israel, which was considered by the Soviet regime as an enemy state. Those were dreadful years for Soviet Jews. In 1952 the anti-Semitism in the Soviet Union was at its peak. One could be fired or get arrested at any moment. My father was about to be fired, too, but Stalin's death in 1953 saved him his job.

In 1956 I applied to enter Moscow State University. It was the year when Stalin was denounced and a temporary relative thaw of the Soviet regime came to the lives of the Soviet people. For the first (and short) time, Moscow State University opened its doors to Jewish applicants. The math department at Moscow State University was one of the top in the world. At my entrance exam in math I was asked to solve eleven problems at the board. I solved only ten. I left the exam being convinced that I had failed and would not be admitted. But I was, and this was a turning point in my life.

I studied mostly mathematics and physics and the required courses in Marxism and Communist Party history. I specialized in probability theory, which at that time was a hot area of mathematics inspired by the great Russian mathematician A. N. Kolmogorov. There were many talented students and young faculty working with him at the time, and mathematical life around him was nourishing and stimulating.

After graduation I worked for four years with Professor Kolmogorov in his applied statistics group and taught in his school for gifted high school students. I was very fortunate to know and work with this great man, who brought up and inspired generations of mathematicians.

Subsequently, I went to graduate school under the supervision of Yakov G. Sinai, one of Kolmogorov's most prominent students. Though very young at the time, Sinai had already made fundamental contributions to ergodic theory, an area of mathematics related to probability theory that originated from thermodynamics and statistical physics. Sinai demanded that his students have a broad mathematical education. This helped me a great deal in my future research. In my thesis I studied the ergodic theory of geodesic flows on negatively curved surfaces, geometrically arising dynamical systems with extremely random behavior.

In 1971, soon after getting my PhD, I emigrated to Israel and began working as a lecturer at the Hebrew University of Jerusalem. Students in Israel were bright and motivated. I immensely enjoyed teaching them. During these years I continued my work on geometric dynamical systems and I corresponded regularly with Rufus Bowen, a young Berkeley mathematician who worked in the same area. Soon I received and accepted an invitation from the Berkeley math department to join its faculty. The mathematical life was flourishing. Almost daily someone would come up with a new idea or make a new discovery.

I made some, too. I was studying the so-called horocycle flows on negatively curved surfaces, which were closely related to the geodesic flows which I studied earlier. I discovered that unlike the geodesic flows of equal entropy, the horocycle flows are statistically very different and are rigidly linked to the geometric structure of the underlying surfaces. It turned out that the ideas I introduced in this work were fundamental and far-reaching, especially for applications to number theory. I first realized this in 1984 at a conference in Hungary, where G. A. Margulis told me that he was influenced by my ideas in his proof of the Oppenheim conjecture in number theory. This was a joyful moment for me. Subsequently, these ideas led me to create the proofs of conjectures of S. G. Dani and M. S. Raghunathan concerning unipotent flows on quotients of Lie groups. It gives me great pleasure to see my theorems so widely applied to solve many other important problems.

For me math is a part of Nature's beauty and I am grateful for being able to see it. Whatever math I happen to teach, I love to communicate its beauty to my students.

YAKOV GRIGOREVICH SINAI

Mathematical physics, dynamical systems, mathematical probability

Professor of Mathematics, Princeton University

My grandfather V. F. Kagan was a very famous Russian mathematician. He was an expert in geometry and wrote several books on Lobachevsky and Lobachevskian geometry. One of his papers written a hundred years ago was recently mentioned in the *American Mathematical Monthly*. At the moment I decided that I would also become a mathematician, my grandmother told me that I should be aware that mathematicians think about mathematics twenty-four hours a day. She asked, "Do you really want to do this?" I thought again and decided I would do it. I try to keep this habit even now.

While I was a student of mathematics at Moscow State University I had several remarkable teachers and advisors. My first advisor was N. G. Chetaev, who was a great expert on classical mechanics. Even then I felt that my main field would be the theory of dynamical systems. My next advisor was E. B. Dynkin, who gave me a very interesting problem. My first publication was the solution of his problem. Then for many years later my teacher and advisor was the great mathematician of the twentieth century, A. N. Kolmogorov. Many people ask how I liked being Kolmogorov's student. The answer is not that simple. Kolmogorov never "played" mathematics with his students. Each problem which he gave led usually to many continuations and fruitful connections. On the other hand, his knowledge of mathematics was phenomenal and he was a great expert in many parts of it. This was very stimulating for all people around him. I learned a lot from I. M. Gelfand, who organized a fantastic seminar in Moscow and also from V. A. Rohklin, who my wife and I considered a close friend.

Now I live and work in Princeton. This is a remarkable place for doing mathematics. I have many friends with whom I have useful scientific contacts, many students and an enjoyable atmosphere in which to work.

BENOIT MANDELBROT

Fractals in geometry, nature, and culture
Sterling Professor Emeritus of Mathematical Sciences, Yale University

Both my youngest Uncle and I were born in Warsaw and grew to be mathematicians. But overly interesting times cursed his late teens and later mine and made us into altogether different persons. He became a focused full-time establishment insider, and I never did.

An adolescent during World War I, roaming around during the Russian Revolution, my Uncle fell in love with classical French mathematical analysis, moved to its source, was soon handed its torch, and kept it burning through both fair weather and foul.

An adolescent during World War II, I found shelter in the poor and isolated highlands of central France. After the war, inherited and trained skill in assisting mathematics by pictures earned me entrance to the famed École Normale in Paris. Instead, I chose to follow a dream—one that my Uncle warned me against as completely childish. I worshipped and wanted to emulate Johannes Kepler's major achievement: taming an ancient plaything—ellipses—to solve an ancient failure of observational astronomy, "anomalies" in the motions of planets.

Against all odds, something of that kind did eventually fulfill my dream. Unwittingly, I faced a task that Plato himself had outlined millennia before our time but that nobody knew how to even start to pursue. Indeed, compared to Euclid, almost every common pattern of nature and culture is not merely more elaborate but altogether more exquisitely irregular and fragmented. For practical purposes, most exhibit a very large—practically infinite—number of distinct scales of length.

The mathematician Henri Poincaré had remarked that one chooses to ask some questions, while other questions ask themselves. How long is the coast of Britain, given that the measured length is increased by ever smaller bays and capes? How to define the roughness of rusted iron, of broken stone, metal, or glass? What shape is a mountain, a coastline, a river, or a dividing line between two watersheds? That is, can geometry deliver what the word seems to promise, namely, truthful measurements of untamed Earth? How fast does the wind blow during a storm? What shape is a cloud, a flame, or a welding? What is the density of galaxies in the universe? What is the volatility of the prices quoted on financial markets? How to compare and hopefully even measure different writers' vocabularies?

Altogether, natural "roughness" raises an astonishing number and variety of questions long left open as hopeless. They challenge standard geometry's conventional view of nature and culture—one that disregards rough forms as formless.

Now, after the fact, my lifetime work can be characterized. I have faced all those old or recent challenges (as well as hosts of analogous ones), in the spirit of Kepler. Half a century before I was born, mathematicians had undertaken what they perceived as a deliberate flight from reality and believed they were inventing what they called "monsters" or "pathologies." Helped by computers, I actually drew those would-be inventions, diametrically inverted their original intent, and showed that a few help handle a host of old concrete problems—the "questions for poets and children" of the kind that I have listed. Playing with the specific "pathologies" that had baffled and stopped my Uncle made me discover what is now called the Mandelbrot set—illustrated here—a form billed as the most complex object in mathematics. In this and other contexts, I extracted from pictures many abstract conjectures that proved to be extremely difficult, motivated a quantity of hard work, and brought high rewards.

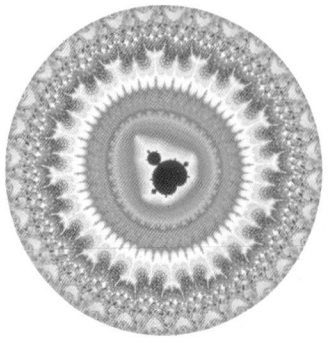

GEORGE OLATOKUNBO OKIKIOLU

Functional analysis

Independent scholar

I was born in Aba in Nigeria in 1941. My mother was a daughter of the Obong of Calabar (literally translated as "King of Calabar"). She trained as a nurse and took up an appointment in a hospital working with doctors and staff from the United Kingdom, the governing country of the then British Empire which included colonial Nigeria in quite "far away" Abeokuta in western Nigeria, where she met my father, a doctor. My mother and her friends suggested the names George and Elizabeth for me and my twin sister after the recently enthroned King and Queen of England.

After early primary schooling in Lagos and at Ibadan, my secondary schooling was at Baptist Boys' High School in Abeokuta, where I lived during term times. I was often away from school to recuperate at home from feverish complaints, but I made sure my performance at school was not below my usual best.

Although my childhood experiences in and around hospitals had made me feel that I would like to grow up to be a medical doctor, my interests in mathematics and the physical sciences had developed, and I pursued those subjects at university, receiving a bachelor of science first-class honors degree. After this first degree, I accepted a research assistantship to write a master's thesis on real and complex variable analysis. I worked on strong lower densities in measure theory and received my master of science degree in 1964.

I presented my first paper on Fourier transforms and Hilbert transforms (and fractional integrals) for publication and applied for a number of assistant lectureship positions in various universities. I commenced an appointment at the University of Sussex in 1965. At that time, our second daughter, Katherine Adebola (now a mathematician!), was born. After the success of my first paper, I was soon presenting other research papers for publication on extensions of Schur inequalities, inversion relations for fractional integrals, and generalization of Hilbert transforms and Dirichlet-type transforms involving trigonometric functions. By 1970, I had published twenty-four papers on various topics in integral operators and was writing my first book, *Aspects of the Theory of Bounded Integral Operators in L_p Spaces*, which was published by Academic Press in 1971. I then continued my studies and received the doctorate of science degree in 1971. There were new appointments to be considered for various positions. I was informed that I was being considered for a professorial position at the University of East Anglia in Britain, but the early notification was not confirmed, and in subsequent years, I was uncomfortable and retired early from university appointments in 1974 to proceed with my personal inventions.

My initial inventions included a proton extractor, electrochemical oscillator, and magnetic-wave generator, but they were not very promising for commercial development, so I considered other new ideas. Two of my main inventive projects include photoconverter technology and television cameras for infrared and other wave forms. Television cameras for various wave forms relate especially to some of my inventions which operate as remote effect devices involving systems for generating pressure waves affecting human subjects. Other notable inventions include polarvisible inscriptions, which are visible only to viewers equipped with suitable polarizer elements; linear and rotary motor assemblies; light-operated photocell-inductor motors for operating electrical generators; hydraulic projections of electrical terminals for various electrical effects; various forms of television assemblies; composite motor-generators for electrical equipment and electrical vehicles; and nuclear fusion systems. By 1975, I had accumulated and published twenty-five United Kingdom patent specifications. As with some forms of industrial developments, productions relating to my inventive projects have been limited by financial considerations.

In 1990, I commenced publication of my books, particularly, *Completion of the Magic Square of Even Order* and *Special Integral Operators, Vol. 1* and *Vol. 2*. I have published two regular periodicals, *Bulletin of Inventions and Summary of Patent Specifications* and *Bulletin of Mathematics,* since 1981.

KATE ADEBOLA OKIKIOLU

Geometric analysis, spectral geometry
Professor of Mathematics, University of California, San Diego

My mother is British, from a family with a trade-union background and a central interest in class struggle; she met my father, who is Nigerian, while both were students of mathematics in London. My father was a very talented mathematician, and after my parents married, he went on to a position in the mathematics department of the University of East Anglia. While I was growing up, the elementary school I attended was extremely ethnically homogeneous. I was unable to escape from heavy issues concerning race, which my mother always explained in a political context. My parents separated after my father resigned his university position to focus on his inventions, and my mother then finished her education and became a school mathematics teacher. We moved to a very cosmopolitan area of London, which was like a new birth to me; it was there that my interest in mathematics really began. I learned mathematics on my own from textbooks, which is perhaps strange given that both my parents were involved in the subject. At the same time, I spent a good deal of time studying art and wanted to follow a career in that direction until I was eventually convinced by my family that I should first work for a mathematics degree to ensure that I could earn a living. I went to Cambridge, which represented a second major change in my life. As I learned more mathematics, I saw that it is an entire world of its own which many people choose to live in, a world in many ways more real than the real world: it feels permanent, eternal, and offers a deep sense of security because nearly everyone who understands it agrees on what is truth.

By the time I had finished at Cambridge, I was very involved with mathematics and did not consider other careers. I moved to UCLA for graduate work, which represented yet another major life change. On graduating I got a position at Princeton University, where I stayed for four years and where I met my husband, who is also a mathematician. After that I spent two years at MIT, and for the past ten years my husband and I have worked at UCSD. We have two children.

My research is in the field of spectral geometry, the study of how the shape of an object affects the modes in which it can resonate. A famous question in the field is, can one hear the shape of a drum? Spectral geometry bridges different branches of science, including engineering and physics, as well as a number of different fields of mathematics. However, quite different sorts of questions are studied within each discipline. I am a mathematical analyst, which gives me an appreciation for the infinite and the infinitesimal. At the moment, one of the things I am working on understanding is the total wavelength of a surface like a sphere or something of greater complexity, such as the surface of a bagel or a pretzel. What is this total wavelength? If you strike a surface it can resonate at any one of a list of frequencies, and the wavelength of the sound produced by the vibration is inversely proportional to the frequency. In the mathematically idealized model there are infinitely many possible wavelengths. The total wavelength should be the sum of all of these individual wavelengths except that this infinite sum equals infinity. Fortunately, a finite number can be assigned to it by a slightly elusive process called regularization. (This process is also used in mathematical physics to mysteriously obtain true answers from formulas which do not really make sense!) I first became interested in the total wavelength as a model related to a question which can be roughly stated as, can one hear the shape of the universe? However, the total wavelength shows up in many quite different areas of mathematics and I am finding these connections intriguing.

Although I cannot claim to find it easy to balance my ambitions in mathematical research with the desire to be a good parent, to be an inspiring teacher, or to effect positive social change in the world, I do feel very fortunate to be able to spend my life tackling these challenges, which are extremely interesting and important to me.

WILLIAM TIMOTHY GOWERS

Functional analysis, combinatorics
Fields Medal
Rouse Ball Professor of Mathematics, University of Cambridge

I grew up in a family of musicians: my father was a composer and my mother a piano teacher. At school I did well in most subjects. Though mathematics was always my favorite, there were several others that I liked almost as much, and it wasn't until I was about eleven or twelve that it became clear that I would be likely to specialize in mathematics, and a few more years after that before I gave up all thoughts of becoming a musician. If I had become one, I would probably have tried to follow in my father's footsteps and write music. And if I had done that, then in some ways my main activity in life would have been similar to what it actually turned out to be. Like a long mathematical proof, a substantial piece of music is a complex abstract entity that must satisfy strict constraints, and creating such an entity involves careful planning on many levels, from the global structure down to the little subproblems that arise when you try to make your higher-level ideas work. My father has always had a keen interest in mathematics, and it feels as though I have taken a path that in another life he might have liked to take himself.

Until I was an undergraduate, I had absolutely no conception of what a career in mathematics would be like, and even when I arrived at Cambridge and started to be taught by professional mathematicians, I had very little idea of what they were doing other than teaching. I ended up as a mathematician not because I decided at an early age that I wanted to be a mathematician—at that stage I didn't even know that such people existed—but rather because at each of the many opportunities that the English educational system gave me to specialize, I was always pleased to do more mathematics and less of other subjects. It helped that I had a succession of unusually good and inspiring teachers who did not confine themselves to the standard syllabus.

It was only once I started a PhD, having cleared all the hurdles I needed to clear to get to that point, that I ever saw what a real mathematical problem was like. Before then the problems I had come across were either famous unsolved problems, such as Fermat's Last Theorem, or carefully designed problems with clever solutions, such as one might find in a mathematical olympiad. But the problems I first worked on, in an area known as the geometry of Banach spaces, were very different. They were not famous, and to solve them it was not enough to spot a clever trick. Instead, I had to use one of the most common methods of mathematical research, which was to take an existing argument that used a technique I would never have thought of for myself and modify it.

As my research progressed, I began to understand that there is more to mathematical skill than problem-solving power: also very important are how one goes about selecting problems to work on and how one persuades others that one's research is interesting. In both cases, it helps greatly if there is a bigger project to which one's work contributes. My current area of research is a relatively new one called "arithmetic combinatorics," which is a very interesting blend of number theory, harmonic analysis, and extremal combinatorics. Arithmetic combinatorics started out as a collection of seemingly isolated problems and results, but gradually it has become clear that these problems and results are related in fascinating and unexpected ways. The bigger project to which I am now contributing is to understand these connections, to develop existing techniques into a more coherent body of theory, and to develop new ideas for solving certain key problems that appear to lie just beyond what the known techniques allow us to solve.

A more direct way to interest others in one's research is to solve a well-known problem, something I have occasionally done. Even here, however, a general research strategy is essential. When one works on a problem that many other people have tried, a little voice in one's ear is constantly saying, "If this approach worked, then the problem would have been solved long ago." And the voice is right 99.9 percent of the time. But if one digs deep enough into a problem, one sometimes manages to identify and isolate a fundamental obstacle to solving it, and just occasionally one discovers that a technique has recently been developed that one can use to get round this obstacle. Such moments of serendipity are rare, but with the help of good research strategy, one can try to make them less so. For me they are the greatest mathematical pleasure.

LENNART AXEL EDVARD CARLESON

Harmonic analysis
Abel Prize
Professor Emeritus of Mathematics, Uppsala University and the Royal Institute of Technology, Stockholm, and former Director, Mittag-Leffler Institute, Stockholm

There are a number of stereotyped ideas about mathematics and mathematicians. I shall look at some of these from my own personal experience.

"There is a small number of people with a very special talent for mathematics."
Certainly you need good intelligence to become a good mathematician. Many people are prepared to use the word "genius" for the student in the class who can solve all problems on a school test. I should like to reserve the word for those with very special insight. In my lifetime I have only met a handful of people like that; they do, however, exist! For the rest of us (in this volume) what really counts is a psychological circumstance. In Stockholm, there is a museum with photographs of all the Nobel laureates. The museum advertises (jokingly?), "Come and see the most stubborn people of the world!" Or consider what Newton said when asked how he conceived the idea of gravitation, "By constantly thinking about it." In my mathematical life I have worked seriously on three different problems and spent five to ten years on each. At times they occupied my mind fully, and one can of course ask if this is a reasonable way to use the few years granted us.

"It is a wonderful joy to work on mathematics and an exceptional satisfaction when you find the solution you have been looking for."

What I said just before could seem to refute this statement, so let me say right away that the assertion is true at times, namely, when things go well. However, most efforts fail and the wastepaper basket is the second (next to pencil and paper) most important piece of equipment of a mathematician. There is an incredible amount of hard work behind the few pages that constitute the final paper. The simpler the paper looks, the better it probably is and the more work it has required. You can be sure it did not come out this way originally. My experience is that the result slowly dawns on you, and it is only after checking and rechecking you realize that you have eliminated all errors. "Eureka" is not a very common word for a mathematician.

"All good mathematics is done by mathematicians less than x years old, x usually taken to be about 30."
Again, there is certainly some truth in this. Let me offer a physiological explanation. The statement is certainly true in athletics. Similarly, in mathematics, for an exceptional accomplishment, you need a very extended concentration, which you cannot achieve when you get old (as I certainly can attest). However, less original work and valuable contributions can still be done after x years, and I definitely don't think one gets more stupid. Groundbreaking results and very complicated ones are a young person's territory, but for results requiring overview and knowledge, we have a chance all through our life.

TERENCE CHI-SHEN TAO

Harmonic analysis, partial differential equations, number theory, combinatorics
Fields Medal
Professor of Mathematics, University of California, Los Angeles

I've always liked math. I remember when I was two or three and I was wandering around with my grandmother. She was washing the windows and just to play a game with me, she'd ask me to pick a number, like 3. I'd use the detergent and she'd spray a big 3 on the window and then clean it. I thought it was great fun. I had workbooks as a kid. They were simple, with equations like $3 + \square = 7$. What's in the box? I thought it was really fun. Math was the only thing that really made sense to me: 3 plus 4 is exactly 7 and that's it. No one will come along later and say actually there's a new fashion and that isn't true anymore. I liked the clarity and thought of math as an abstract game to play. It was only later that I realized how it related to the real world and how it's used for all kinds of things.

I grew up in Australia. My parents had me tested as a child, and once they realized I had some ability, they arranged special classes for me. I skipped some grades, though in a staggered way. For instance, when I was in eighth grade, I'd do some classes in English and physical education but I was taking twelfth grade mathematics and eleventh-grade physics. When I was in twelfth-grade in high school, I'd take college classes in math. My mother had to pick me up from high school and drop me at the local university. It was very complicated. In some classes I'd be with people roughly my own age and in other classes I'd be with people five years older. Most of my classmates were much taller and bigger than me. It was a shock when I taught my first class at UCLA at age twenty-one because for the first time ever I was the oldest person in the room.

I study the prime numbers. These are numbers which can't be divided by any other number except themselves and 1, like 2, 3, 5, 7, 11, and so forth. One of the things I showed with Ben Green is that you can find a certain type of pattern inside them known as an arithmetic progression. Somewhere inside these primes you can find five primes or ten primes or twenty primes or as many primes as you want, which are equally spaced. Prime numbers have been studied for three thousand years, mostly out of curiosity. The average person in the street doesn't need these prime numbers for anything. But the funny thing is that about thirty or forty years ago, it was discovered that prime numbers were very good for cryptography; in fact, they were much better than the other codes that people had invented. Nowadays, if you use an ATM machine or a credit card over the Internet, they scramble all your data by a certain code which is based on properties of prime numbers, because they are one of the most secure codes we know.

Mathematics can be like archaeology. You might find a corner of something and decide it's of interest. Then you dig somewhere else and you find another corner that looks very similar and think there may be some deep connection. You keep digging and finally discover the structure underneath. You have a thrill of discovery when something finally makes sense.

I work with a lot of very good and intelligent people and I've learned a lot from them. But it doesn't pay to take the attitude that you have to be a super genius in order to succeed. If one springs a math problem on a lot of really good mathematicians unexpectedly, they'll initially be slow in responding. You can watch them thinking. After five or ten minutes, they'll come up with some really good suggestions. They might not be very fast but they can be very deep. Everyone's got different skills. It's like athletics. There are sprinters and there are marathon runners. A sprinter would be horrible as a marathon runner and vice versa, but they're both good talents.

There are a lot of problems I'd like to solve in my lifetime, but many of them are like cliffs and I have no obvious way to get up them. I'm working on things that are more within my reach and I'm hoping to accumulate more tricks and tools and insights. Then I'll go back to the problems I really want to solve and see if anything has changed. Occasionally they budge a little. It's a bit like fishing. You can be a good fisherman and you can be in a place where there are lots of fish but you still have to wait for the bite.

ROBERT CLIFFORD GUNNING

Complex analysis
Professor of Mathematics and former Dean of the Faculty, Princeton University

I have been privileged to live the life of an academic mathematician, and a privileged life it is. It has an invigorating annual renewal: the departure of one group of undergraduate and graduate students whom one has tried to provide with a knowledge of and intuition about some parts of mathematics, with a sense of the excitement and challenges of mathematics, with at least some responses to the questions they have raised or should have raised, and with the encouragement to continue to learn and use mathematics. Then there is the arrival of a new group of undergraduate and graduate students, having various degrees of eagerness and various expectations, to continue the process with fresh minds and new interests. After each intensive academic year there is the opportunity for regrouping and renewal over the summer: the time to review what has been done over the past year, to digest and organize what was learned, and to commit to paper those ideas or calculations that have matured; the leisure to read more extensively in the mathematical literature; and the freedom to ponder new directions or new problems on which to concentrate.

Mathematics itself is a delightful field, both stable and ever changing, with challenging depths and fascinating breadth. It is perhaps the only really cumulative human endeavor: new concepts arise and old ideas can be reworked, expanded and generalized, but none are lost and all are incorporated in the expanding body of mathematical knowledge. Archimedes' technique for calculating volumes of regular solids by slicing was incorporated and extended as Cavalieri's principle in the development of calculus in the seventeenth century and extended further as Fubini's theorem in the development of general theories of measure and integration in the twentieth century; and who knows where it will appear in the future. The basic ideas were never lost but rather were generalized and embedded in more extended mathematical structures. Mathematics is also incredibly broad, with an ever expanding range of results and problems, so that a mathematician is never at a loss for new areas to examine and new problems to consider. One never teaches the same material over and over again but always finds new ideas, new applications or organization of older material, new relations with other fields, new and different problems to which to apply known techniques or techniques to attack known problems; and there is such a breadth of material that one can pursue ideas without the pressure of working on almost the same problems as a large fraction of other mathematicians. The recognition of new structures, the understanding of what really is going on in a proof, the delight in seeing at last the solution to a problem after sometimes long and agonizing periods of contemplation, of full wastepaper baskets, and of sleepless nights during frustrating periods of apparent lack of progress: all these are what makes mathematics such a challenging but supremely joyful endeavor.

ELIAS MENACHEM STEIN

Harmonic analysis
Albert Baldwin Dod Professor of Mathematics, Princeton University

When I was very small, I became fascinated with the idea of perpetual motion. At the age of five I thought I had invented such a machine. I elaborated on this idea and imagined many variants of it. My parents didn't know anything about science, but they humored me. When I got older I realized it probably wouldn't work, but it was comforting to maintain the illusion that I had some special talent and I might do something great.

When I was ten, in 1941, I came to America from Belgium because of the war. Shortly thereafter I became very interested in chemistry and then physics. Later I took a very inspiring course in plane geometry in high school, which convinced me that mathematics was what I wanted to do. I was also lucky because at Stuyvesant High School, there were other kids of my age who were fascinated by mathematics. Later I chose to go to the University of Chicago over Harvard because I found it difficult to get up in the morning, a habit that became more ingrained when I was a graduate student. I usually slept until noon. The University of Chicago had a system, unique then, where classroom attendance was not required and grades of courses depended only on final exams at the end of the year. Although my choice of universities was not made for the most intelligent reasons, it turned out to be very fortunate. In fact, Chicago was a mecca for great scholars and scientists, and what I learned there from my teacher Antoni Zygmund and friends and colleagues has been a lasting influence in my life.

I got my first job at MIT, where I stayed for two years. Then I returned to Chicago as a faculty member for three years before I went to Princeton. Chicago was a great center of analysis. I was at home there, so leaving its warmth was not without some hesitation. Arriving in Princeton, I felt a little like a pioneer settling in a territory that seemed a bit unfriendly. But things soon changed.

I work in a field called harmonic analysis. Mathematics has a long history and the main subjects are sometimes hundreds of years old. This area started at the end of the eighteenth century but its nature has changed a good deal, even in my lifetime. I initiated some new viewpoints and exploited novel connections of that subject with a number of other areas. While I'm very proud of my contributions, I realize that nothing essential is really unique to an individual.

Some people work on mathematics because of particular applications outside of mathematics. I'm not one of those. I'm more interested in it for its own sake. There is another distinction I would make. There are some who work on specific hard problems because of their challenge and so are motivated by a great desire to solve these riddles. There are others who strive to see various interconnections and seek to develop broad points of view. The latter is more my style.

What is mathematical activity like? It is hard to put this in words, but I would say that in part, it seems to me most like art. There is a great deal of freedom of what you might want to do, and you judge the interest of your work by some inner aesthetic feeling in addition to the joy it gives you. On the other hand, in mathematical research one cannot escape the hard constraints of rigor and relevance, and ultimately its worth is decided by science in the ripeness of time.

JOSEPH JOHN KOHN

Several complex variables, partial differential equations
Professor of Mathematics, Princeton University

I was born in Prague, Czechoslovakia, and lived there until the age of seven. We migrated to Ecuador in 1939, three months after the Germans occupied Prague. My maternal grandfather was a well-known lawyer and he had a keen interest in mathematics and the sciences. I still remember that when I was five he explained to me how to estimate the height of trees using a marked walking stick and how to tell the time of day from the position of the sun. My father was an architect and from an early age he got me interested in perspective, geometry, and art. Since childhood I have been fascinated by mathematics and by mathematical reasoning in science.

During my first three years in Ecuador, we lived in a provincial town (Cuenca) and my education was very rigorous and old fashioned. In particular, in mathematics it was mostly memorizing various algorithms such as the "rule of three," the "rule of nine," a method for taking square roots, etc. I was always intrigued by this and worked hard at understanding why these methods worked even though the attitude of my teachers was that these rules were a given and they should be taken on faith. During the next three years in Ecuador we lived in Quito, the capital of Ecuador, and I went to an American school, Colegio Americano de Quito, where the curriculum was the same as in the United States. The school was much less demanding and the mathematics was really watered down. The contrast between these two schools was striking. In Cuenca we were required to learn an enormous quantity of material by rote; in the American school there was much less formal study and a great emphasis on self-expression and on extracurricular activities.

After elementary school my education continued in the United States. I went to Brooklyn Technical High School, where I had a number of inspiring teachers. My study of mathematics and science was not confined to the classroom. I was a member of the math club, the math team, and the junior astronomy club of the New York Museum of Natural Science. I decided that I would study mathematics, which was a difficult decision because it was not clear how one could make a living as a mathematician. I went to MIT, where I majored in mathematics and I took courses from some remarkable mathematicians, such as Witold Hurewicz, Norbert Wiener, John Nash, and Norman Levinson. In addition to the ideas and techniques that I learned in these courses, I got insights about the different ways that mathematical research can be approached.

I went to graduate school at Princeton University. The Princeton mathematics department had many of the world's leading mathematicians and a wonderful graduate program that emphasized research. The standard American graduate education in mathematics in the 1950s consisted of three years of very demanding course work followed by a thesis. Princeton's graduate program was unusual: the courses were quite informal, no grades were given in them, and the students were encouraged to search for a research topic early. Thus there was a clear distinction between the undergraduate regime that consisted of learning specific material to be tested on and the graduate program of independent study to develop research interests.

I had been (and still am) fascinated by the interplay between partial differential equations and complex analysis. Given my interests, I made the best choice of a thesis adviser. Donald Spencer was very enthusiastic and supportive; he encouraged me to pursue my ideas and suggested directions of research. Most importantly, he was a role model: his enthusiasm, tenacity, dedication, and high standards have been guides to my mathematical development.

I was very fortunate that my first job was at Brandeis University. It was a young department in the process of building up and I found it very exciting to be part of these efforts. At Brandeis I was encouraged to work on significant problems; quality was emphasized over quantity. So I had the opportunity to develop an ambitious long-term program of research without the common pressure of frequent publication.

In 1968, I moved to the Princeton University mathematics department. I continued my research in an ideal atmosphere. Several of my colleagues were working on problems closely related to my own work, and I had a number of truly talented students who made remarkable contributions to the problems that I was interested in.

The highlights of my career were the moments when, after many frustrating efforts, I made progress in solving a problem or in understanding some feature that enabled me to advance in my research objectives. It is a fascinating never-ending pursuit of goals: as soon as a question is answered, others arise and the chase continues.

CHARLES LOUIS FEFFERMAN

Fourier analysis, partial differential equations
Fields Medal
Herbert E. Jones, Jr., University Professor of Mathematics, Princeton University

As a little kid, I wanted to know how rockets work and borrowed a physics book from a library. I didn't understand one word. My wise father explained to me that the book was full of math, which I hadn't studied.

I set about reading math textbooks, starting with fourth-grade arithmetic. After I got through calculus, my father took me to our local university, the University of Maryland, for tutoring. That was the start of my relationship with the University of Maryland. They were wonderful. It's a big state school, but I had the feeling that their whole math department was giving me private tutoring. I attended Maryland as an undergraduate. It was illegal since I was only fourteen years old, but the chairman of the math department threatened to resign if the university didn't admit me. You wouldn't be interviewing me today if it hadn't been for them.

I went to Princeton as a grad student. It was a great stroke of luck for me to study with Eli Stein, a great mathematician and perhaps the best teacher of math I've ever known. Eli's teaching and example are still a major influence on my work.

I would like to describe two of my contributions. The first is a connection between Kakeya sets and Fourier analysis. Kakeya sets are strange shapes in the plane. One can turn a 1-inch-long needle through a full 360 degrees, keeping the needle entirely inside a Kakeya set; yet the area of a Kakeya set is as small as you please. Fourier analysis is the study of how complicated vibrations break up into simple ones. For example, the complicated motion of a violin string is made up of a fundamental note, a first overtone, a second overtone, and so on. The sound of the violin string is degraded if the high frequencies are removed.

In part, that's because the violin string is one-dimensional. A photograph is a two-dimensional image, also built up from simple pieces analogous to the fundamental note and overtones of a string. Because a photo is two-dimensional, it may be out of focus yet come into sharp focus when its high frequencies are removed. That's because of the existence of Kakeya sets. I discovered this in the 1970s. Kakeya sets in dimension higher than two continue to present challenging problems. The photos in this book are in perfect focus.

Secondly, I've spent many years on mathematical problems about atoms. Any quantum mechanics textbook explains why one electron and one proton combine to make one hydrogen atom. The textbook won't tell you why a billion, billion, billion electrons and a billion, billion, billion protons combine to make lots of hydrogen atoms. That's a much harder problem, which entails a lot of math; the full solution isn't yet known. I made a contribution by reducing the problem to an estimate for the energy of the system.

I don't choose problems; they choose me. A question will grab hold of me and I feel compelled to think about it for years or decades. On a typical day, I get no ideas, but on a good day, I get a wrong idea. Wrong ideas are ingredients in the pot. Add enough ingredients and the stew cooks. With luck, it tastes good.

At Princeton, I usually teach a graduate class (often on my own work) and an undergraduate class (often elementary calculus). When research is going badly, it's pleasing to think that I'm doing something useful by not giving my freshmen a hard time.

ROBERT FEFFERMAN

Harmonic analysis, partial differential equations, probability
Dean of the Physical Sciences and Max Mason Distinguished Service Professor of Mathematics, University of Chicago

My mother, who was raised in Germany, attended schools featuring exceptionally strict discipline and particularly poor instruction in mathematics, and she thoroughly hated the subject. My father was an economist who earned his PhD without taking so much as a calculus course because he was advised by his teachers that economics had nothing to do with math. Having consistently excelled in math courses in high school, he had loved and respected the subject as much as any other student and had always wished to take up calculus on his own. My parents had two children and both became mathematicians. I think that in no small measure, my father's attitude and experiences with mathematics influenced us in our intellectual mission, while our mother could only look on in amazement.

My brother, Charles, served as a great role model for me, and I remember greatly enjoying mathematics by watching his wonderful career and his enthusiasm, even while my own early experiences in school were not very pleasant. My own love of mathematics did not develop until late in high school, when I had an outstanding calculus teacher. It was in this class that I decided to seriously consider becoming a mathematician, and the beauty and depth of the subject became extremely clear. I remember having some of the best educational experiences of my life reading about function theory, and I entered college very much determined to pursue the subject as a major. At the University of Maryland, my professors, especially John Horvath and Nelson Markley, showed great talent and patience in giving me the background I would need to thrive in graduate school. When I arrived at Princeton, I believe I was well prepared to profit from the extremely rich environment there.

There was really little doubt in my mind, when entering Princeton, whom I would ask to be my thesis advisor. E. M. Stein was an exceptionally talented researcher with a very attractive and broad set of interests in mathematics and who was equally talented and charismatic as a teacher.

It was wonderful to learn that modern harmonic analysis, which had developed out of the study of trigonometric series, was so deeply connected to such fascinating topics as set theory and number theory, complex function theory, gambling games and probability, and the most basic concepts of real variables, such as questions of how to split a function up into large and small parts. The connection with differential equations, present in the theory since Fourier's discoveries, underscored the applicability of this important branch of mathematics. I think these connections illustrate one of the very most appealing features of harmonic analysis and of mathematics in general: its dual nature as beautiful art form, and its most serious source of fundamental applications to virtually every area of human knowledge.

Of particular interest to me was an area of harmonic analysis invented by Alberto Calderón and Antoni Zygmund at the University of Chicago: singular integrals. Eli Stein, who had received his graduate training at Chicago, had written a classic text on the subject, which guided a great many happy students through this lovely part of analysis. He emphasized that certain objects called "maximal operators" were at the center, controlling the way these singular integrals behaved, and I became involved in trying to better understand these maximal operators. Soon after starting this kind of investigation, I left graduate school at Princeton for the University of Chicago. Several mathematicians in this area had formulated questions relating to an extension of Calderón–Zygmund theory to singular integrals with higher-dimensional singularity sets. Even the simplest case of this was completely mysterious at the time, and this was the product theory. This theory presents the kind of challenges that one would face if one were to wear two watches in order to keep time, and the times registered on the watches were different and completely independent of one another. To add to this already rather confusing situation, Lennart Carleson had given a counterexample which suggested that the usual Calderón–Zygmund results were not going to go over to this new setting in a straightforward way. Fortunately, due to the efforts of a number of people, the product theory of singular integrals is now in great shape, and we understand extremely well how it fits into the classical theory. One final area that particularly interests me is the application of harmonic analysis to the theory of elliptic equations, especially when the coefficients of the equation in question are very rough.

All in all, I have been extremely fortunate to have the kind and patient support of my family, teachers, and colleagues, and this is a good place to say "thank you!" to all of them.

YUM-TONG SIU

Several complex variables
William Elwood Byerly Professor of Mathematics, Harvard University

Born in China in 1943, I spent my childhood in Macau and teenage years in Hong Kong. After my undergraduate education at the University of Hong Kong, I went to the University of Minnesota for a master's degree and got my PhD from Princeton University in 1966. Since 1992, I have been the William Elwood Byerly Professor of Mathematics at Harvard University and served as chair of its mathematics department between 1996 and 1999. Before joining Harvard in 1982, I held faculty positions at Purdue University, the University of Notre Dame, Yale University, and Stanford University.

Although my mathematics career spans forty-two years, as a child I never dreamed of being a mathematician because my first passion was Chinese literature, especially classical poetry. It was not until I dabbled in assembling radios that I began to develop an interest in science and mathematics about the time I started junior high school. I used to hunt for discarded radio parts in flea markets and get great satisfaction in using successfully Kirchoff's laws to make very simple modifications in circuit diagrams to fit the parts I managed to get. Later I discovered that I like theoretical sciences more than time-consuming experimentation.

Mathematics appeals to me because of its beauty, its clarity, its logical certainty, and its universality. It transcends language and cultural barriers. It extracts the logical commonality of structures of nature in complete clarity beyond any doubt.

My mathematics research has been in the field of several complex variables, a branch of analysis, very closely linked to geometry. Calculus deals with real variables, representable as measurements. A complex variable allows the use of complex numbers including the square root of -1. The field of several complex variables deals with more than one single complex variable and provides the most natural platform to study and understand equations and the geometries of their solutions which arise in physics, astronomy, engineering, and other applied scientific fields.

Sometimes people wonder how one could find satisfaction in doing fundamental research guided only by intellectual curiosity and beauty without any specific immediate application and timeline of payback in mind. Mathematicians feel that a true and deep understanding of structures of quantities, symmetry, and space will eventually lead to really novel useful applications which are deeper and more far-reaching than those spawned by mission-oriented research. On the practical side, mathematics does not require any high-cost outlay. With the ever increasing use of computers it is getting into the quantitative side of practically all fields, many of which, up to the recent past, have had nothing to do with it.

Looking back at my career, I find one of the most critical elements fostering it is an intellectually stimulating environment. As a graduate student, I benefited from discussions with fellow students. Mentors and role models such as Robert Gunning, my PhD thesis advisor, Eugene Calabi, Hans Grauert, and Joseph Kohn have definitely shaped my research agenda and my view of mathematics.

LOUIS NIRENBERG

Analysis, partial differential equations
Professor of Mathematics and former Director, Courant Institute of Mathematical Sciences, New York University

My love of mathematics began when I was a child. My father tried to teach me Hebrew, but I foolishly resisted, so he got a friend to give me private lessons. But he liked mathematical puzzles, so much of each lesson was spent on them. I went to high school in Montreal during the Depression. To be a high school teacher was considered a desirable job, and I had excellent teachers, particularly the physics teacher, who had a PhD. I decided I would try to study physics.

In college I majored in math and physics, with the intention of becoming a theoretical physicist. I graduated at the end of the Second World War, and by pure luck, Richard Courant, at New York University, offered me an assistantship to do graduate work in mathematics. My idea was to get a master's degree and then go on to study physics. I stayed with mathematics, but I have enormous admiration for physicists.

Most people think that mathematics is a dead subject. They don't know that new developments are being made all the time and that it's enormous fun to work on them.

People ask, "What's required?" Naturally, talent helps, but curiosity and perseverance (to the point of stubbornness) in wanting to know if some conjecture is true or not, and why, is necessary. The same is true in many creative fields.

My work is mainly in partial differential equations, which describe many phenomena in physics and economics as well as in such mathematical areas as geometry and complex analysis. My doctoral thesis was on an unsolved problem in geometry, which required new results in showing the existence and uniqueness of solutions to these differential equations. Obtaining such results often requires finding detailed estimates on the sizes of the functions and of their derivatives, and that leads to the careful examination of inequalities. I must say that I love inequalities and am often excited when I am told of a new interesting one. Using partial differential equations to attack problems from other fields of mathematics and science involves studying properties of solutions of these equations, for example, to see whether there are useful symmetries of these solutions. Some of my work has involved establishing such symmetries for some general classes of equations.

I only wrote one paper on what might be called applied mathematics. (In general I don't believe in the distinction between pure and applied math.) It concerned fluid dynamics. There is a long-standing problem in that field about whether solutions of the fluid dynamical equations remain smooth as time progresses or whether they might develop singularities. With two collaborators I proved that if singularities do develop, their one-dimensional measure is zero, for instance, they cannot fill a curve.

I very much enjoy working with other people and 90 percent of my papers are joint work. Some mathematicians learn mainly by reading. I've always found reading math difficult: I've learned mainly by listening to people speak about their work. Some mathematicians develop new theories. Some are mainly problem solvers and work on a given problem. I am of the second kind, but I have the highest respect for the first.

Traditionally, mathematics problems arise from questions in nature, mainly from physics. But many questions come out of mathematics itself. The past few decades have seen remarkable new interactions with physics. Physicists have come up with new mathematical ideas, and mathematicians have made contributions in physics. In addition, results in one branch of mathematics have been found to have deep, often astonishing, consequences in another. It's all fantastically exciting.

WILLIAM BROWDER

Algebraic topology
Professor of Mathematics, Princeton University

Asked the question, how did three brothers all end up becoming mathematicians? as I often am, I have no ready answer. Genetic predisposition is belied by the fact that our parents had no relation to mathematics, our mother having a law degree from St. Petersburg, and my father largely self-educated, leaving school in the third grade, reading widely, and earning a degree in law, as well, by mail. Though he never practiced, the degree stood him in good stead in defending himself against the government in various prosecutions, after he had been thrown out of the Communist Party after many years as chairman in its most successful era.

All three of us were bookish, surrounded by books of all types and levels. Felix was a child prodigy, reading at a very sophisticated level from the age of four and terrorizing all his grade school teachers with his breadth of knowledge and sophistication. Being the youngest of the three, I encountered many teachers who had had either Felix or Andy and as a result treated me with the greatest respect and care.

We all played chess at a reasonable level, and we read the newspapers with eagerness, especially during the Second World War. Asked what I wanted to be when I grew up, I progressed through architect (based on Lincoln Logs and Tinkertoys), mechanical engineer (Erector sets), chemist, and finally physicist, after the excitement of the atom bomb. It was in the pages of the *New York Times* in August 1945 that I first read the description of the atom and nuclear fission and learned the atomic number and weight of the isotopes of uranium. I had read some wild science fiction before that, but this was a wilder reality.

In high school, I enjoyed the physics and chemistry courses and the picture of the logical and beautiful construction of the physical world that was displayed. I read popular science books, and was sold on physics. The math courses were usually boring and computational, with not much beauty, with the exception of a one-term course in Euclidean geometry.

Arriving at MIT, I had several shocks. First, I was no longer the smartest one around. I met numerous students who were much more sophisticated and well-read in science and math. And there were required courses in physics and chemistry which had an important laboratory component. I was all thumbs in the lab (two left ones at that).

In the second year, I took a mathematical physics course, and there I discovered a mysterious new phenomenon. Some of the students had something called "physical intuition," which enabled them to give strange and wonderful answers to questions, which were greeted by the professor with delight but made no sense to me at all. At the same time, the professor was making a computational hash of some mathematics that was being explained in a very beautiful and motivated way in a math course I was taking. I began to understand that my brain was not constructed to do physics as it was really done, but was much more fit for mathematics.

In graduate school at Princeton I discovered the beauty of algebraic topology, in which Princeton was the leading center in the world. My advisor, John Moore, suggested a very interesting problem, on which I began to read. Then some months later he gave me a proposed solution of tremendous beauty and scope. I tried to work out the details of his suggestion, but progress was slow. Then just before I left to take my first job, he discovered that the idea was wrong. I went off to Rochester with only one small result toward a thesis, to a department where I would have no one in my field to talk to. This in retrospect was a blessing of great proportions.

After six months of depression and buoyed by the possibility of a much more interesting job at Cornell, I decided to simply sit down and try to write the simplest things I could deduce about the problem. Suddenly I saw a whole new aspect of the situation and, with energy and enthusiasm, slashed away at a thesis.

I had learned an important lesson. It was the joy of getting a new idea, of finding something that no one had before thought of, of working out my own way to new results. I could never take mathematical advice; it did not stimulate me. Only my own peculiar point of view could get my blood rushing. I could read other people's work, enjoy it, and be stimulated by it, but only in so far as I could get my own point of view could I make real progress. This has always been my greatest strength, and also my greatest limitation.

In an age of "directed research," as many of the scientific authorities would have it, I would have shriveled and died as a scientist. As I tell my students, point of view is everything, and, as in writing, one must find one's own voice to really contribute.

FELIX E. BROWDER

Functional analysis, partial differential equations
University Professor of Mathematics and former Vice President for Research, Rutgers University;
and Max Mason Distinguished Service Professor Emeritus of Mathematics, University of Chicago

I was born in Moscow, Russia in July 1927 and was brought to the United States at the age of five. I am the son of Earl Browder, the expelled general secretary of the American Communist Party. My father didn't graduate from primary school. His father was an unemployed schoolteacher and trained his children at home, but my father essentially taught himself. My father opposed World War I and was the leader of Socialist antiwar agitation in Kansas City, Missouri. He was jailed in 1917–1920 for his opposition to the war. Over the course of his lifetime, my father amassed a library of ten thousand books.

My mother had an initial interest in astronomy but received a law degree from the University of St. Petersburg. This was very difficult before the Russian Revolution because she was Jewish, and Kharkov was the only city where she could practice law. She became secretary to the mayor who, unlike her, was not a Bolshevik. My parents met in Moscow in 1926 when my father was visiting the Lenin School, a special school for aspiring Communist leaders. He was working for the Kremlin in the Profintern, which was the Communist International of Trade Unions. He was there as a representative of the Communist Trade Unions in the United States.

My two brothers, Andrew and William, and I are all mathematicians. My brother Bill and I are the only pair of brothers that are members of the National Academy of Sciences. We were also presidents of the American Mathematical Society. In the 1970's and 1980's, for eleven years I was chairman of the math department at the University of Chicago. During part of that period Bill was the chairman at Princeton, and Andrew was chairman of the math department at Brown University. I have no clear idea why we were all drawn to mathematics.

I graduated from Yonkers High School in 1944, then entered MIT and I graduated in mathematics in 1946. I was one of the top five contestants in the William Lowell Putnam Competition, a national math contest for undergraduates. I entered Princeton in 1946 and at the age of twenty, in 1948, I received my doctoral degree in mathematics with a thesis on nonlinear functional analysis and its applications. This area and partial differential equations have been my focus in the sixty years since, in particular nonlinear monotone operators from a Banach space to its dual.

From 1948 to 1951, I was one of the first two Moore Instructors at MIT. During a period of difficulty in getting mathematical employment, which lasted until 1955, I had an instructorship but was denied any permanent or long-term position at MIT, despite the recommendation of the department. In 1953, I was awarded a Guggenheim Fellowship. At the same time, I was drafted into the United States Army. In the army, I was classified as a security risk and eventually received a trial for this status, for which I was finally acquitted. In 1955, I left the army and became assistant professor at Brandeis University. In 1956 I went to Yale, where I moved through the academic ranks. Then in 1963 I moved to the University of Chicago, where I remained for twenty-three years. In 1986 I retired from the University of Chicago to become a Vice President of Rutgers University. In 1999 I received the National Medal of Science in mathematics and computer science.

You may be wondering why I am sitting in what appears to be an empty room. It is empty because we are about to move into this new house. One of the reasons we chose to move is that I needed more space for my thirty-five thousand books. The library has a number of different categories. There is mathematics, physics and science as well as philosophy, literature and history, with a certain number of volumes of contemporary political science and economics. It is a polymath library. I am interested in everything and my library reflects all my interests. All my life, this has been a singular point in my career in mathematics. I know very few mathematicians, with the recent exception of Gian-Carlo Rota, who are interested in everything.

ANDREW BROWDER

Functional analysis
Professor Emeritus of Mathematics, Brown University

Many mathematicians, perhaps most, knew from an early age that mathematics was the most interesting thing in the world and can hardly imagine wanting to do something else. I'm one of the exceptions.

In the spring of 1955, with the truce in Korea still holding, the Eisenhower administration decided to reduce the size of the military. One of the measures adopted was to offer early release from service (up to three months) to anyone attending graduate school. At this time, I was a private at Fort Dix and looking forward to civilian life: I applied to graduate schools for the first time and was lucky to be accepted by MIT. To tell the truth, I didn't really expect to stay in school very long, but rather, to my surprise, I found myself more and more interested in mathematics.

Many years ago, when I called myself a mathematician, I managed to prove a few theorems. I found all these theorems to be quite interesting, and so did a few others. I also wrote two books, which a number of people claimed to find valuable. I taught well over a hundred courses, some of which I found to be interesting and enjoyable, some pretty depressing, most somewhere in between. The students had parallel experiences. I enjoyed a couple of years as a Miller Fellow in Berkeley, and a couple of years in Aarhus, Denmark. Over all, it was a good experience. One might say I owe it all to the U.S. Army, and of course the GI bill.

Some view mathematics as a science, some as an art; to others, it is primarily a sport. My own main sport was always chess. My father taught me the game when I was six, a friend of the family gave me a chess book when I was eleven or twelve, and after that I was hooked. I never attained any serious skill, though I was once the Brown University champion and can boast of a 50 percent score against grandmasters (I participated twice in simultaneous exhibitions given by grandmasters and managed a draw each time). Every ten years or so, the addiction would strike, and I would spend exorbitant amounts of time playing the game and replaying the games of the professionals. After a year or so, the fever would pass. It was finally the advent of computer programs that could always beat me easily that cured me of this malarial addiction. For a while I turned to the game of Go (weiqi). This game has very simple rules but is extremely difficult; so far as I know, computers have not been programmed to play much beyond the beginner level. I barely got above that level during that brief period some twenty-odd years ago when the Brown math department experienced a Go craze.

Concerning many issues, I like what Ludwig Wittgenstein once wrote, "Wovon man nicht sprechen kann, darüber muß man schweigen," which can be translated into English as "Whereof one cannot speak, thereof one must be silent."

CATHLEEN SYNGE MORAWETZ

Partial differential equations, fluid flow

Professor Emeritus and former Director, Courant Institute of Mathematical Sciences, New York University

One of my daughters said to me that the problem of being a mathematician is that you're on stage all the time in the sense that you're constantly trying to achieve something in the form of proving a theorem. That's unending. You compete against yourself as well as others and it provides a special fascination in life.

In my youth, there were not many women who wanted to try this. However it was, in a way, a natural profession for me. My father, John L. Synge, was a mathematician who went back and forth from Ireland to Canada. He was on the mathematics faculty of the University of Dublin and then of Toronto, and I always heard about mathematicians. The general idea of my parents was that I was quite smart but that I should not go into mathematics. They thought I was too flighty. My father also had a problem about having a fellow mathematician in the family, so I was not particularly encouraged. When I was in high school, I had a teacher of mathematics who was much more knowledgeable than the average math teacher. He organized a session after school to help students get scholarships to the university, but in retrospect, I believe, he did it for me. I ended up getting a very nice scholarship to go to the University of Toronto. The setup there was such that the only way I could take the scholarship was to go into the program of mathematics, physics, and chemistry and stay there. I went into that program and I was stuck with those subjects. After about two years, I didn't like it very much but I stayed a third year. This was during the war, when there was a lot of restlessness. I had a boyfriend who was in the navy and I decided that I should do something for the war. I ended up working in a ballistics proving ground near Quebec City. I enjoyed myself very much and got a sense that I really liked proving things. I returned to college to finish my last year. I then ran into Cecilia Krieger, a mathematician whom I had known most of my life. She asked me what I was planning to do when I graduated, and I told her I was planning to go to India as a teacher. She was horrified and told me I had to go to graduate school. I told her I did not know how to do that and she immediately arranged for me to get a fellowship. I went to MIT because Caltech did not take women. At MIT I got my master's degree in mathematics after a short side effort in electrical engineering. I also married Herbert Morawetz, whom I had met in Toronto and who had been transferred to New Jersey. So I looked for a job in the New York area. Through my father I met Richard Courant at NYU, and he hired me to solder electrical connections on an early computer, but instead I edited his book with K. O. Friedrichs on compressible flow.

At NYU I took more courses in mathematics and fell in love with the subject and the student atmosphere. I was then and still am more interested in something that has an application, such as my work in transonic flow. Suppose you have an airplane flying along. The sound speed is a local phenomenon and depends on the pressure. It is quite possible to have a bubble in which the flow is supersonic, that is the local speed is greater than the speed of sound, and elsewhere the flow is subsonic. Subsonic flow is very smooth, but supersonic flow may have shock waves that create drag forces on the wing. There was a lot of curiosity in the '50s about whether you have to have a shock wave or not. I managed to settle some questions there. That was a theorem with a real application. I also worked on collisionless shocks, which occur potentially in thermonuclear reactions but actually in outer space and in the solar system. "Collisionless" means that the molecules travel enormous distances before they hit each other. The usual idea is that the shock is really a smooth transition, and it's about as wide as the mean free path of the molecules or closely related to that. If the collisions take place very far apart, then how can you get something that looks like a discontinuity? I worked on that problem for a number of years.

From 1951 to 1960, Courant generously allowed me to work part time and in that way I was able to raise our four children. I was often warned that they would turn out badly but the opposite was true.

PETER DAVID LAX

Partial differential equations
Abel Prize
Professor of Mathematics, Courant Institute of Mathematical Sciences, New York University

Like most mathematicians, I became fascinated with mathematics early, about age ten. I was fortunate that my uncle could explain matters that puzzled me. Mathematics had a deep tradition in Hungary, going back to the epoch-making invention of non-Euclidean geometry by John Bolyai, a Hungarian genius in the early ninteenth century. A journal for high school students, and contests, were instrumental in identifying talented young people early and they were nurtured intensively. I was tutored by Rózsa Péter, an outstanding logician and pedagogue. Her popular book on mathematics, *Playing with Infinity*, is still the best introduction to the subject for the general public.

At the end of 1941, I came to the United States with my family, sailing from Lisbon on the last boat to America. I was fifteen years old. My mentors wrote to the Hungarian mathematicians who had settled in the States, asking them to take an interest in my education. I finished high school and enrolled at New York University to study under the direction of Richard Courant, widely renowned for nurturing young talent. It was the best decision I ever made.

At age eighteen I was drafted into the US Army. After basic training, and six months of engineering studies at Texas A&M, I was posted to Los Alamos, a part of the Manhattan Project. It was like living science fiction. Upon arrival I was told that the entire community was feverishly working to build an atomic bomb out of plutonium, an element that does not exist in nature but was manufactured in an atomic reactor in Hanford, Washington. The bomb would put an end to the war. By any measure it was the biggest scientific enterprise of all time, led by some of the most charismatic leaders of science. Los Alamos, this supersecret Shangri-la, was located high up on a mesa, surrounded by unbelievably beautiful mountains with caves of ancient American Indians only a hike away.

After a year at Los Alamos I came back, demobilized to New York University, finished my college education, and obtained my PhD in 1949. I returned to Los Alamos for a year and continued to spend many summers there as a consultant. The experience of working as part of a large scientific group decisively influenced my mathematical outlook, as did the emerging discipline of scientific computing, which Los Alamos had pioneered. In 1950, I became a junior member of the mathematics department at NYU. I remained there for fifty years, basking in the collegial, noncompetitive atmosphere of the Courant Institute.

Mathematics is sometimes compared to music, but I find a comparison with painting better. In painting there is a creative tension between depicting the shapes, colors, and textures of natural objects and making a beautiful pattern on a flat canvas. Similarly, in mathematics there is a creative tension between analyzing the laws of nature and making beautiful logical patterns.

Most of the work I have done begins with problems suggested by physics, such as the propagation of sound waves, the way they are scattered, and the formation and propagation of shock waves in fluids. But the mathematics had to be beautiful. Many of these problems have led to intriguing questions in pure mathematics.

Mathematicians form a closely knit, worldwide community. Even during the height of the Cold War, American and Soviet scientists had the most cordial relations with each other. This comradeship is one of the delights of mathematics and should serve as an example for the rest of the world.

ALAIN CONNES

Noncommutative geometry
Fields Medal
Professor of Mathematics, Collège de France, l'Institut des Hautes Études Scientifiques, and the Ohio State University

I believe that mathematics is one way the human mind can create concepts. In many ways mathematics plays a role that philosophy could have played in creating concepts that then can be used in the real world. It takes time for them to evolve and be used in the real world, but the real factory is mathematics. Its concepts have to do with shape and abstract things among others, and they are much more subtle and diverse than numbers. This is probably something that the general public does not realize. Mathematicians use numbers only when they are needed. One could say that the idea of energy comes from physics, but in fact, it originates in mathematics. Mathematics is the ultimate language in which there is a distillation of abstract ideas that become very precise and can then be used in different fields. At the same time, mathematics can be very tough because it's resistant. It's a very stubborn reality; you cannot do whatever you want. It is scary. One shouldn't be scared. There's a beautiful saying by Alexander Grothendieck who said, "To be afraid of making a mistake is the same as to be afraid of the truth."

There's a story of a friend's child that shows the essence of mathematics very clearly. At age five, he was on the beach with his father. He had been quite ill at age three and the father was always a bit worried about his health. For one hour, the child sat on the beach quietly looking pale. The father was worried. Then the child came to his father and said, "Dad, there is no largest number." The father was amazed. The father, who was not a mathematician, asked, "How do you know?" The child gave him a proof. We hear a lot of nonsense about children learning how to count on their fingers. Here you have a little child of five years old who found, on his own, a true mathematical fact and he found it in his brain, not in a book. He discovered it by pure thought and found the proof. This is the essence of mathematics. Of course there is a tradition. There are plenty of books, and things that we learn do not evaporate because they have a proof. On the other hand, mathematics is something with which you can have direct contact without any intermediate tool. This is the most striking feature of mathematics. You can be completely by yourself and you can still think about mathematics. You wouldn't necessarily do the mathematics that is important now because in order to do that you have to have read the latest things. I'm not saying you should work in isolation. You wouldn't go anywhere if you did that. But what I am saying is that when you get started, to really become a mathematician, the key step is to realize that at some point you have to stop reading books. You have to think on your own. You have to become your own authority. There is not an authority to which you have to refer. At some point you have to realize that whether something is written in a book or not doesn't matter. What matters is whether you have a proof and whether you're sure of it. The rest doesn't matter. This can happen in a child very early.

With regard to my own work, my thesis, you have the Cartesian point of view, which is ordinary geometry. Here you have coordinates and so on. But, there are spaces that are more complicated because they are spaces where you not only look at the points of sets but you also look at the relations between the points. These new sets, sets with relations, can be described by algebras, but these algebras are noncommutative. This was at first found by physicists and it can be explained extremely simply. When you write a word on a piece of paper, you have to pay attention to the order of the letters. A friend wrote me an email at one point and for some time I couldn't make sense of it because in four places I couldn't identify the meaning. It took me some time to realize it was my own name but written with a different order of the letters. When one does ordinary number calculus or ordinary algebra, as it's called, then you can permute the letters. The order of the letters doesn't matter. If you write 3 x 5, it's the same as 5 x 3. In physics, it's been found that this is not the case when you look at microscopic systems. You have to be more careful. You have to pay more attention. What I found in my thesis was that if you look at algebras where you pay attention to the order, time emerges. Time emerges from this noncommutativity: the fact that you pay attention to the order of the letters. This led me to my work on the classification of factors. After working on this for ten years, I developed in full a new geometry called "noncommutative geometry," in which one refines all the usual geometrical ideas and applies them to the new spaces. These spaces have amazing properties that generate their own time. Not only do they generate their own time, but they have features which enable you to cool them down or warm them up. You can do thermodynamics with them. There is an entirely new part of geometry and algebra that is related to these new spaces, called noncommutative geometry, on which I have been working essentially all my life.

ISRAEL MOISEEVICH GELFAND

Group representations, analysis
Associate Faculty Member in Mathematics, Rutgers University

I do not consider myself a prophet. I am simply a student. All my life I have been learning from great mathematicians such as Leonhard Euler and Carl Friedrich Gauss, from my older and younger colleagues, from my friends and collaborators, and most importantly from my students. This is how I continue working.

Many people consider mathematics to be a boring and formal science. However, any really good work in mathematics always has in it beauty, simplicity, exactness, and crazy ideas. This is a strange combination. I understood early on that this combination is essential from the example of classical music and poetry. But it is also typical in mathematics. Perhaps it is not by chance that many mathematicians enjoy serious music.

When we think about music, we do not divide it into specific areas as we often do in mathematics. If we ask a composer what is his profession, he will answer, "I am a composer." He is unlikely to answer, "I am a composer of quartets." Maybe this is the reason why when I am asked what kind of mathematics I do, I just answer, "I am a mathematician." I want to remind you that when the style of music changed in the twentieth century, many people said that the modern music lacked harmony, did not follow standard rules, had dissonances, and so on. However, Shoenberg, Stravinsky, Shostakovich, and Schnittke were as exact in their music as Bach, Mozart, and Beethoven.

In the 1930s, a young physicist, Wolfgang Pauli, wrote one of the best books on quantum mechanics. In the last chapter of this book, Pauli discusses the Dirac equations. He writes that the Dirac equations have weak points because they yield improbable and even crazy conclusions:

1. These equations assume that, besides an electron, there exists a positively charged particle, the positron, which no one ever observed.

2. Moreover, the electron behaves strangely upon meeting the positron. The two annihilate each other and form two photons.

And what is completely crazy:

3. Two photons can turn into an electron-positron pair.

Pauli writes that despite this, the Dirac equations are quite interesting, and especially the Dirac matrices deserve attention. I was lucky to meet the great Paul Dirac, with whom I spent a few days in Hungary. I learned a lot from him. I asked Dirac, "Paul, why, in spite of these comments, did you not abandon your equations and continue to pursue your results?"

"Because they are beautiful."

Now there is a radical perestroika of the fundamental language of mathematics. During this time, it is especially important to remember the unity of mathematics, to remember its beauty, simplicity, exactness, and crazy ideas.

The text above is adapted from the introduction to the talk of Israel Gelfand, "Mathematics as an Adequate Language," presented by him at the International Conference on Unity of Mathematics held in Cambridge, MA, in 2003 in honor of his ninetieth birthday.

VAUGHAN FREDERICK RANDAL JONES

von Neumann algebras, geometric topology
Fields Medal
Professor of Mathematics, University of California, Berkeley

I grew up in New Zealand, one of two children in a family with no academic ties whatsoever. My father had briefly begun to study law, but the Second World War intervened and he never returned to study. I do recall that my mother was good with numbers, and from an early age I was eager to learn about arithmetic. I remember making up my own multiplication tables if I was sent to my room for misbehaving.

My formal education was normal enough for New Zealand, where the schools at that time were of exceptional quality, and I began to study mathematics and physics at Auckland University when I was seventeen. My real calling began when I started to do some research after my master's degree. I was thrilled by it, as opposed to taking classes that I had come to find rather boring. The actual research I was doing was in a somewhat marginal area of mathematics, but it is amazing how much those ideas have turned out to be useful in my now more central mathematics. Although I missed out on the usual scholarships to study abroad, the Swiss government came to the rescue of my research career by offering me a scholarship to study in Switzerland. The offer came with the attractive condition that I spend three months learning French in the Swiss Alps before beginning my scientific studies. I was to remain six years in Geneva and have visited there many, many times since. I met my wife while skiing in the Alps.

My PhD was marked by the contact with my advisor André Haefliger and Alain Connes, whose work knocked my socks off. I just had to contribute something along those lines and I mastered a very small part of Connes's oeuvre and made a little progress. But it wasn't for another year or so that I struck out on my own and did something really original. I got very lucky for although my result, known as "the index theorem for subfactors," looked very technical, it turned out over the next few years to have lots of connections with many different areas of mathematics and physics. Perhaps the biggest impact has been in knot theory.

How to determine when two knots in a closed string are essentially the same is a difficult question, with the first rigorous answers arising only at the beginning of the twentieth century. My index theorem for subfactors led me to discover a way of calculating a "polynomial" from the subfactors to discover a way of calculating a polynomial from the diagram of a knot—a polynomial that has been rather useful in fields as diverse as quantum field theory, mathematical biology (DNA knots), and quantum computing. The mathematics behind this polynomial is relatively easy, but its profound meaning is still somewhat mysterious. One does not know how to connect it satisfactorily to other more geometric approaches to knots. But there are many conjectures.

When not involved in mathematics I tend to like to do sports, including golf, squash, racquetball, tennis, and skiing. I used to play rugby and cricket when growing up in New Zealand and still love to watch rugby. But my main sporting passion in the last fifteen years has been windsurfing, and more recently kiteboarding, which I find a bit easier on my aging joints. In an amusing connection with my academic life, I have run into lots of knotting questions associated with these sports and sailing in general. I am probably the only kiteboarder around who actually thinks in terms of braids and their inverses when connecting the lines to my kite.

Music is another interest. I like to sing and all three of our children have been involved in music. There are a lot of ingredients in common between mathematics and music. My life remains full of surprising connections between its different facets and I expect to be surprised many more times.

SATHAMANGALAM RANGAIYENGAR SRINIVASA VARADHAN

Probability, applied mathematics
Abel Prize
Professor of Mathematics, Courant Institute of Mathematical Sciences, New York University

While growing up, most Indian children of my generation thought they wanted to become doctors, engineers or elite officials of the administrative services of the Indian government. My initial desire was to become a doctor. This changed abruptly when as a ten-year-old, I visited a college fair at the local medical school. The anatomy exhibits of real human body parts were so discomforting that I then switched to engineering as a more acceptable alternative. I was always good in mathematics at school. Even though this only meant that I could add, subtract, multiply, and divide rapidly without making mistakes, it somehow seemed to imply an aptitude for engineering!

We had an excellent mathematics teacher in high school who changed my view of the subject. He convinced us, a small group of his good students, that mathematics is not unlike the game of chess. I was good at chess as a child, having learnt the game from my mother when I was three years old. There are rules to be followed and you play to reach specific goals. Mathematics, like playing chess or solving a puzzle, can be fun!

I still had no comprehension of what it meant to be doing research in mathematics as a career. You could teach the subject at high school or college level. While the science curriculum at school introduced us to modern discoveries and research, there was no counterpart in mathematics. When it was time for my undergraduate studies, I chose statistics for my major because it was close enough to mathematics while offering the prospect of a career in industry. My father, who was a school principal, was fortunately very open-minded and did not discourage me from opting out of medicine, engineering, and administrative services. I ended up in graduate school in statistics, still a bit lost about exactly what I was going to do. I was fortunate enough to get to know fellow graduate students who knew what they were doing and introduced me to the wonderful world of modern mathematics. I got hooked!

I have spent all of my professional career in the United States and have enjoyed it very much. Interaction with others has always been an important source of ideas for me. Working on a mathematical problem is not unlike putting together a complex structure or puzzle. One quickly finds most of the pieces and reduces the problem to finding one or two key pieces that are needed but cannot be readily found! It may take months or years or an entire lifetime to find the last key piece and when it is found, perhaps from a spark provided by listening to somebody in a different context, the problem is solved. This sense of satisfaction cannot be described in words!

MARIE-FRANCE VIGNERAS

Algebraic number theory, Langlands program
Professor of Mathematics, Institut de Mathématiques de Jussieu, Paris

I was raised in Senegal. I mention it only because I received a prize years later by proving that "one cannot hear the shape of a drum": in a mathematical sense there exist distinct drums which cannot be distinguished by their sounds. The question was raised while I was attending a conference in California in 1977 and it reminded me of nights in Africa when I listened to Senegalese people playing drums and dancing outside our home; I had tried to guess what the instruments were from their sounds.

Happy coincidences like this one are often responsible for theorems. Ideas come while lying in bed or sitting in a lecture or in a concert, when there are no worries, no teaching or cleaning, no stress. Think of yourself in a forest. You enjoy the beauty of nature and it is not cold, but light becomes dim and it is time to leave the forest. You try a tiny path but it ends quickly. You walk back and try another one; they all look the same and it is darker. You stop and stay motionless. You wait and wait, with your senses alert to see the invisible, to feel the undescribable, to listen to the silence. And it happens suddenly: one direction becomes more dense, or more luminous. To experience this intense moment is the reason why I became a mathematician. Energy, concentration and hard work are needed to write proofs. You have to pay attention. Mistakes can easily slip into them. As mathematicians, we play and dream but we don't cheat. You can't cheat in mathematics. Truth is so important. To solve a problem with a proof is exciting and rewarding because it is true forever.

I became a mathematician by luck (starting with a good teacher in Dakar, Damon, and the excellent French education of the time) and I am living a simple life. I teach for four months and do mathematics during the rest of the year. I love both. Mathematics is the deepest thing in my life and it influences me strongly. I feel I am different from, let us say, my neighbors, but not so much from historians, writers, poets, and artists.

MICHÈLE VERGNE

Group representations, differential geometry
Director of Research, Centre National de la Recherche Scientifique, France

What did I do in my life as a mathematician? I could look at my list of publications and discuss some of my old results. However, the past counts for nothing. If I am not able to prove something new now, what I did before is worthless. So here I am, day after day, working for hours pursuing some infinitely distant goal.

I am trying to "understand." I am not trying to discover something new, but rather see the "essential reasons" why some results are true. I return to the source, in an attempt to discover "the mother of all formulae." Other mathematicians' new ideas and results are irritating. I would desire very much to show that there is a simple reason why "all of that" is true (at least when I was young I had that arrogance).

Sometimes I succeeded in finding "higher reasons" why a result was valid: an idea springs up from my past work and lands just there in front of me, ordering me to do something. Why was it so easy to understand the Plancherel formula for nilpotent groups and so hard for reductive groups? I was puzzled by this question for a long time.

Suddenly, an inner voice speaks to me and tells me it is not harder. And the voice continues to give me orders: "just add terms and employ the Poisson formula." The invisible protagonist disappears from the scene, leaving me all the work. Wondrous miracle, I see the bridge of light and the work is easy to do. I am enchanted. The result becomes a logical consequence of another fact I knew, and in a blitz, I can annex a small part of mathematics to "my world." But soon, this fleeting feeling of satisfaction disappears and I realize that there are more profound cases that my insights are unable to explain: I "explained" Harish Chandra's Plancherel measure for reductive groups, so what about Plancherel measure for symmetric spaces? To deal with this more general case, my new idea is powerless. I am unable to prove this, so the value of what I proved before is nullified.

Today I can see a dim light on a problem that has been on my mind for a long time. This is the assertion: quantization commutes with reduction. It was a beautiful conjecture of Guillemin–Sternberg, which was clearly true, but revealed itself hard to prove in general. I was able to prove an easy case. A much more difficult case was then proved by another mathematician ten years ago, using surgery. For me, this method via cuts is ugly. I would have liked to prove this conjecture with my own methods. Long after the full proof was found, I kept reorganizing my own arguments in all possible ways. If I repeated them over and over, the difficulties were bound to disappear. But they did not. These ceaseless failed attempts left a scar. I do still hope to discover where exactly the difficulty was, and today I feel I know the very small hole where the difficulty was hiding. I think it can be grasped easily. Then, maybe, I will be able to formulate and prove the theorem in a much more general way. True, for that I need someone else's idea, but just recently, I used a brilliant idea of one of my students to explain a very similar phenomenon. I believe it can also be used to understand this case. Anyway, I will try. Tomorrow.

ROBERT PHELAN LANGLANDS

Automorphic forms, group representations

Hermann Weyl Professor Emeritus of Mathematics, Institute for Advanced Study, Princeton

Although there are at present many occupations that require a good deal of skill and training in advanced mathematics, mathematics itself is still often regarded as a curious profession demanding singular talents and a singular personality. My own character—apart from a certain tolerance of solitude, even a preference for it—has always seemed to me to be quite ordinary. As a child, I was more apt at arithmetic calculations than my classmates, but my geometric intuition was not remarkable, and I was never fascinated by puzzles or intellectual games. The preference for solitude was perhaps acquired during an early childhood passed with little company but that of a mother and one younger sister, later two, in a tiny settlement on the western shore of Canada. On my reaching school age, the family returned to a more populated region with a parochial school where the nuns, encouraging a clear aptitude for reading and arithmetic, had me skip a class.

A little later, elsewhere, I found myself with classmates who were older than I, many several years older and with no academic future. The boys could work in the bush as loggers, returning home from time to time with money and leisure to squander. I was still too young for that, although I started working after school—but not as a logger!—on Saturdays and in the summer, until the age of twenty, when I became a graduate student. There were no mechanical aids at the time; everything, no matter what its weight, was carried by hand. The many hours of physical effort as a youth meant that my body has lasted much longer than a sedentary occupation might have otherwise permitted. Above all, work and solitude, the two conditions of a mathematician's best hours, became at an early age my frequent companions.

My decision to attend university was accompanied by a rediscovered taste for reading, and a collection of brief biographies of those thinkers regarded as decisive by some of the smaller socialist parties of the 1930s came into my hands: Albert Einstein, Sigmund Freud, Karl Marx, Charles Darwin, and James Hutton, among them. Certainly, I was always tainted by a certain ambition and desire to be important that could attach itself to no particular ability or skill. However, some ability at basic arithmetic and logic I certainly had, and I quickly discovered a genuine passion for speculative thinking of all kinds. These biographies of savants and scientists revealed an unfamiliar, unexpected possibility to me. I opted for the adventure of mathematics and the even more glamorous physics. It turned out over time that I had a severe disability as a physicist. I was fascinated by mathematical explanations of natural phenomena, examined their logic with great care, but did not have the right eye for the phenomena themselves, so my focus was off. In mathematics, it was also frequently off, but never irretrievably.

As an undergraduate, I was largely preoccupied with acquiring basic mathematical skills. It was only when I went to Yale as a doctoral student that I began to think uninterruptedly about mathematics. In the first few years after Yale, I took as models for emulation three mathematicians; Harish-Chandra, Alexander Grothendieck, and A. N. Kolmogorov. With Grothendieck and Kolmogorov, it is more a respect for their goals than a full understanding of what they achieved. Both Harish-Chandra and Grothendieck were engaged in constructing theories. They had in common a trait that, oddly enough, is very rare among mathematicians but that commands an unconditional respect. Not satisfied with partial insights and partial solutions, they insisted—not so much in the form of intentions or exhortations as in what they brought to pass—on methods that were adequate to establishing the theories envisaged in their full natural generality. Harish-Chandra's supreme technical power revealed itself in a novel field, infinite-dimensional representations. I myself found my way to it early, and for a time, until I accepted my own limitations, was persuaded that any worthwhile mathematics had to be on the level at which he functioned. Grothendieck, in contrast, entirely reshaped a more mature field, algebraic geometry, one that had seen almost two hundred years of development by some very great mathematicians. I could admire the quality he shared with Harish-Chandra but it is only slowly over the years, as my mathematical activity acquires a more reflective, more historical tinge, that I am coming to appreciate the extent and depth of his reformulation of geometry.

What I have achieved has been largely a matter of chance. I thought about many problems with no success. With other problems, there was the occasional inspiration—indeed, some that astound me today. Certainly the best times were when I was alone with mathematics, free of ambition and of pretense, and indifferent to the world.

JEAN-PIERRE SERRE

Algebra, geometry, number theory, topology
Fields Medal, Abel Prize
Honorary Professor, Collège de France

I prefer to close my eyes when I think about mathematics. The best work is done by night, in half sleep. Sometimes I go to bed thinking, "Ah, I have a nice lemma to prove—or disprove." (Should I explain what a lemma is? A mountain climber needs holds to get from one level to the next one. Lemmas are the holds of a mathematician.) Of course one has to write things down later, if only for publication. Sometimes you then find that what you have thought was wrong, but that's rare.

My thesis is a typical case. There was a simple-looking but rather powerful new idea (the "loop space fibering," found at night, on a train). This basic idea was not enough: there was a technical part which required a rather difficult lemma. During three days I could only see the proof of that lemma when I was flat on my bed, my eyes shut. After that, I understood it clearly enough so that I could write it down and my thesis was essentially done.

At that time, I was working in the branch of mathematics called topology. Two years later I started doing something else: several complex variables (the favorite topic of my thesis advisor Henri Cartan). It did not last long. After one year, I was attracted by algebraic geometry, and then number theory, group theory, etc. The end result is that, even now, I am not an expert in any subject!

I feel I should tell you about the several conjectures I made in the last fifty years. What is a conjecture? It is something that you cannot prove but that you expect to be true and interesting. I made quite a few of these, including some completely wrong ones when I was less than thirty years old. I got more careful with age. Several of these conjectures have been much studied by a lot of people. Among them are the ones on Galois cohomology which are called "conjecture I" and "conjecture II." Conjecture I is now a theorem (proved three years after I made it). As for conjecture II, it is still open after forty-five years, but most special cases have been proved. Perhaps it will turn out to be false in the other cases? I don't think so, but what I really hope for is that it will be decided: yes or no!

If you look on the Web at "Serre's conjecture," you shall probably find a different one (on Galois representations) which I made in the early '70s (and in a refined form in the mid-'80s). It became very popular for two reasons: it is related to Fermat's last theorem (bad reason) and it is a first step towards the "Langlands program in characteristic p" (good reason). It looked out of reach until about five years ago, when suddenly somebody had a brilliant idea and solved a big part of it. Now, with the help of several different people, it seems that the conjecture is dead: it has become a theorem! Indeed, in a few weeks I am going to a two-week conference near Marseille in which the proof will be summarized and explained (even two weeks are not enough to give complete details).

At the time I made this conjecture (in its refined form), I had decided to write it in a setting with which I was familiar and which could be explained easily. But, on a higher level, I knew that it should be done in a different way. The two ways were of course similar, but not a priori equivalent. There was a conflict between my conscious decision of making things "easy" and my unconscious feeling that it was not "the right way." This conflict haunted me; it made me very unhappy. There was even one horrible night where I had the impression that there were two parts of my brain which were fighting each other and spinning endlessly. Then, a few months later, I found an example showing that the two points of view are not equivalent, and the correct one is not the one I had chosen. But I also saw that, in all the really interesting cases, they are equivalent. Curiously, finding this "counterexample" made me incredibly happy: the two sides of my brain had reconciled. Happy End.

ADEBISI AGBOOLA

Number theory, arithmetic geometry
Professor of Mathematics, University of California, Santa Barbara

Unlike many other mathematicians that I know, I was not enamored of mathematics as a young child. I found it dull, confusing, and difficult. I was interested in, and good at, most subjects in school, but I had no interest at all in mathematics—despite being constantly told by my parents and teachers how important it was to acquire a good knowledge of the subject—and for years I regularly failed almost every mathematics examination that I took. I remember on one occasion when I was very young, I decided that I hated mathematics so much that I was determined to think of a career that I could pursue that would involve the use of no mathematics whatsoever. My parents were understandably quite skeptical about this, and when I triumphantly announced "wood cutter," they pointed out to me that this would not do because I would in fact have to measure the wood.

This situation changed completely when, at about the age of twelve or so, in my school library, I came across one of the volumes of the Life Science Library (published by Time–Life International) entitled *Mathematics,* by David Bergamini. This was unlike any other mathematics book that I had seen before. It was essentially an account of the history of some of the main ideas of mathematics, from the Babylonians up until the 1960s, and it captured my imagination and made the subject come really alive to me for the very first time. After reading this book, I knew that this was what I wanted to spend as much of my time doing as I could. I became fascinated by mathematics, and I found that I enjoyed it enormously. This is what led to my deciding to become a mathematician.

Later on, after I had completed my undergraduate studies at Cambridge and it was time for me to think about beginning research towards a PhD, I became interested in number theory. For me, one of the most beautiful things about mathematics is how several different notions or ideas that at first sight have nothing at all to do with each other can in fact be shown to be closely related, sometimes in very profound and mysterious ways. This phenomenon occurs frequently in number theory, and it is one of the main attractions of the subject. It has been suggested that in some respects, pure mathematicians have more in common with creative artists than with hard scientists. I think that many number theorists especially, myself included, would agree that there is a great deal of truth to this statement.

I am sometimes asked, especially by students, how I go about deciding what topics or problems to work on. This is a hard question for me to answer precisely. Some mathematicians explicitly decide that they want to solve a particular problem, or they set out to develop a large research program in a certain area. I do not work in this way. In my case, what tends to happen is that I find that I am curious about certain things at any given time and I want to understand them better. (Sometimes these are things that are well understood by some other people, but not by me.) I go to talks and seminars, I read papers, I talk to people and I ask myself questions, I play around with examples, and in this way one thing leads to another and new ideas emerge. I should also point out, however, that most of the ideas that I have and the things that I try do not work, and I suspect that the same is probably true of many other mathematicians. Of course this just means that perseverance is a crucial part of the entire process, and that it is very important not to just give up too easily!

MARCUS DU SAUTOY

Number theory

Professor of Mathematics, University of Oxford

My math teacher pointed at me during a lesson and bellowed, "du Sautoy! I want to see you after the class." I was twelve. I was terrified. Had I done something wrong? When the bell rang for the end of the class he took me round the back of the maths block. "Now I'm in real trouble," I thought. But then my teacher proceeded to explain that he thought I should find out what mathematics is really about. According to him, the mathematics we were learning in the classroom wasn't real mathematics. He pointed me in the direction of a number of books including *A Mathematician's Apology*, by G. H. Hardy. He suggested I read Martin Gardner's column in *Scientific American*. It was a revelation. I read about prime numbers, the language of symmetry, the strange world of topology. I experienced the thrill of my first proof. Hardy wrote about mathematicians being makers of patterns, patterns that had to be beautiful. It was like I'd been learning a musical instrument, only allowed to play scales and arpeggios, and for the first time someone had played me a piece of real music.

From that point on, I knew I wanted to understand this new world, to inhabit it, to create inside it. My mathematical investigations have been inspired by those early encounters. I work in the border between number theory and group theory. Number theory explores the properties of things like prime numbers, wild numbers that seem to have no patterns to them. Group theory is the language of symmetry. My research looks to unravel what symmetries are possible, both in the physical world around us and also in the higher dimensional worlds that mathematicians love to inhabit. To navigate this world of symmetry, I use a tool from the world of number theory called a zeta function, which was originally used to unravel the secrets of prime numbers.

Doing mathematics is like taking a drug. Once you have experienced the buzz of cracking an unsolved problem or discovering a new mathematical concept, you spend your life trying to repeat that feeling. My most exciting moment was the discovery/creation of a symmetrical object that connects the world of symmetry with the fascinating theory of elliptic curves. Mathematics for me is about finding these interesting connections, like tunnels that take you from one part of the mathematical universe into a seemingly unrelated area.

Being a mathematician is about creating new mathematics but it is also about communicating those new ideas to others. I am passionate that mathematics shouldn't just be for those inside the ivory tower of academia. To pay back what my teacher did for me when I was at school, I spend some of my time trying to bring maths to the masses. Through books, newspaper articles, radio, and TV, I am trying to communicate what it is I find so fascinating about my subject and why I have dedicated my life to solving mathematical problems.

PETER CLIVE SARNAK

Analysis and number theory

Eugene Higgins Professor of Mathematics, Princeton University, and Professor of Mathematics, Institute for Advanced Study, Princeton

During elementary and high school, mathematics was my favorite subject, in part because it was one of the few subjects that came easily to me. However, outside the usual interests of any teenager, my passion was tournament chess where I enjoyed success at the junior and senior levels in southern Africa. My father was very supportive of my (and my brothers') involvement with chess while we were kids, but far less enthusiastic about my running off to Europe at age seventeen to try to make it as a chess professional. He insisted that I first get a university education and that defined my future.

In my first year at the University of Witwatersrand in Johannesburg, with its enthusiastic and excellent young math faculty, I was exposed to modern mathematics (and applied mathematics), in particular to works of such mathematicians as Carl Friedrich Gauss, Johann Lejeune Dirichlet, and Bernhard Riemann. The beauty and depth of their discoveries convinced me that I wanted to learn and understand more and, if possible, to contribute to the development of modern mathematics. I took all the mathematically related courses I could find. In hindsight, one advantage an undergraduate education offers at a mathematically remote place is that it provided me a broad mathematical foundation.

After completing my undergraduate degree, I left South Africa for Stanford University to study with Paul Cohen. Word of his genius and personality had reached all corners of the mathematical world and he lived up to these stories. In particular he imparted to me the view, which I carry to this day (and pass on to my students), that mathematics is a unified subject and even with all the specialization that has occurred, one can still work effectively in different fields within mathematics. Often the most interesting breakthroughs come precisely from such a broad view and interaction between fields.

I have worked in areas ranging from analysis to number theory and mathematical physics. A recurring theme throughout this work is the role of symmetry and group theory. The modern theory of zeta and L-functions, which has its origins in the works of Dirichlet and Riemann, has far-reaching applications to prime numbers, to Diophantine equations such as the solution of quadratic equations in several integer variables, to combinatorics and theoretical computer science, and even to the understanding of the quantizations of certain arithmetically defined chaotic Hamiltonian systems. Finding and exploiting these applications in order to solve basic problems of these types has been one of the major thrusts of my work.

I have worked mostly in collaboration with others, which has allowed me to do things that I could not have done myself. Collaboration is also a means to digest new fields and techniques in a hands-on and one-on-one basis. In particular, I learned much from my joint works with Ralph Phillips, Ilya Piatetsky-Shapiro, Nicholas Katz, Henryk Iwaniec, and Alexander Lubotzky. There is another nice psychological aspect to collaboration. I find, as I think do most mathematicians, that when doing research one is stuck at least 95 percent of the time. One has to live with this, and having collaborators to share in both the frustration, as well as the elation if and when a breakthrough comes, smooths things out. Luck has played a part in a number of these breakthroughs, in the sense that a critical insight was stumbled upon, even by a misunderstanding, while trying to do something quite different.

I have been blessed with many good PhD students, a number of whom have been quite outstanding and who have made their marks in the field. I have often learned as much from them as they have from me. Students have played a big part in my being able to realize many of my research dreams.

The continued support of my immediate family through the ups and downs of working on elusive mathematical problems has been critical in allowing me to keep at it. As many have said before me, I feel fortunate to be able to earn a living doing something that I enjoy and for which I have yet to lose any enthusiasm.

GERD FALTINGS

Number theory, algebraic geometry
Fields Medal
Director, Max Planck Institute for Mathematics, Bonn

I grew up in a coal-mining town in the German rustbelt. My father was a physicist working as an executive in the chemical industry and so I got interested in physics. After some time, I came to mathematics because I found it more interesting. Everything in mathematics is very logical, and that appealed to me. I like it when something is definitely right or definitely wrong.

I studied in Münster, which is near my hometown. I had a very good teacher who encouraged me to study Alexander Grothendieck's work on algebraic geometry, although this had somehow gone out of fashion. Even now some people consider it as far too abstract; however, I have profited from this solid foundation throughout my career.

I work in number theory and proved, at age twenty-eight, something called the Mordell conjecture, which had been an open conjecture since 1924! Because of this, practically overnight I went from nobody to a star of the profession. Even better, while proving the conjecture, I found a number of interesting problems which I had solved "by hand" but were more satisfying when I worked out a more complete theory. A few years later I tried to understand a paper by Paul Vojta and ended up with a completely new theory. It is my experience that I do not need a strategic plan but that interesting problems and new methods tend to come up by themselves. I rarely make conjectures myself. Usually I have an idea that might work in some cases and I try it out. Sometimes it works. Often it doesn't and then I have to start anew.

The work I do is very rewarding because I find myself back in the product I produce. It's very satisfying if you can make your own project and finish it, having accomplished something that others couldn't. Your name is then attached to the accomplishment, which is more satisfying than most people experience in their work. I think I am very privileged.

I have a wife and two daughters, who are now eighteen and twenty. They're all mathematically inclined. We like to do puzzles and we sometimes play cards together. They enjoy playing computer games which they sometimes show me and get me to try them, too. We like to go to the opera and ballet, or at least watch them at home on DVD.

ENRICO BOMBIERI

Number theory
Fields Medal
IBM von Neumann Professor of Mathematics, Institute for Advanced Study, Princeton

I grew up in Montepulciano in central Italy, south of Siena. It is a small town surrounded by walls and situated on top of a hill with many houses and six or seven churches. I went to school there and had many friends. I liked to take walks in the countryside, explore caves, bicycle, play soccer, and read mathematical books. My father was in the banking business but he also had been interested in mathematics, so there were a few mathematical books in the house, accessible to the nonexpert. When I began my interest in mathematics, my father did not object. The only thing he said was, "If you want to do mathematics, you should know that you will never be able to make much money. But whatever you do, follow your inclination and do it as well as you can." He encouraged me and when I asked him to find certain books, he helped me. By the time I was fifteen, I was doing research in number theory.

Number theory is studying the integers (1, 2, 3, 4, and so on) and how they relate together. For example, there is the famous triangle of Pythagoras with sides 3, 4, and 5 that determines the right angle. There are other numbers that satisfy this type of relation, and this would be one aspect of number theory. Another example is the prime numbers. They are difficult to study, but they are very important because they are the building blocks of all the numbers using multiplication. Number theory is a very old part of mathematics, going back to the early Chinese and Greek cultures. I always thought that number theory was too abstract for application, but I had to change my mind seeing how the modern theory of prime numbers has found significant practical applications, as in ensuring security in communications. The lesson to be gained from all this is that knowledge, even when it is not immediately motivated by short-term gain, is always very precious.

I was able to solve, sometimes in collaboration with various authors, some problems that had been open for a long time. Probably my most important discovery is a result about the distribution of prime numbers that turned out to be very useful in other questions and still finds applications today. People ask me why I became a mathematician. The answer is, simply put, that I really like mathematics. I consider myself very lucky that I can do what I like for my work. For many people, work is just something you do to make a living. In such cases, the compensation may be success, more money, or meeting interesting people. For me, I will do mathematics no matter what, simply because I like to think about mathematics.

There are no formal classes at the Institute for Advanced Study, where I teach. We get young postdocs fresh from receiving their degree. It is important for them to expand their horizon and go beyond delving into their thesis topic. They have to learn other things as well and our role is to guide them and help them to become independent. Independence is very important. They must learn to judge by themselves what is interesting and worth doing, not just listen to the advice of others. When they come to me and ask what they should do next, that is the sign that they are not independent.

Good science is always created. One needs to imagine how things may be and proceed from there. It is critical to be flexible and not to have preconceived ideas, not to force things to look the way you would like them to look. A danger in creative research is to get excited by certain ideas, overvalue their significance, and try to make them fit within what one knows. This is what I call "shoe-horning," attempting to fit everything into too small a box. The big discoveries always have a quantum jump with respect to established knowledge, be it mathematics or other sciences. We can also learn a lot from studying the work of our predecessors. It is said that we all stand on the shoulders of a few giants, but let us not forget that we all depend on the humble contributions of many: those who are not architects and engineers but are workers able to put together the bricks on which science is founded. I think that the strength of science comes from the collective contribution of all scientists, and the total is much more than the sum of the single parts. I am confident that mathematics, and all science as well, still has a bright future in front of it.

VISCOUNT PIERRE DELIGNE

Algebraic geometry, modular forms
Fields Medal
Professor Emeritus of Mathematics, Institute for Advanced Study, Princeton

I was born in Brussels. I am told that when I was little, I surprised people by understanding what negative numbers were. Why were they surprised? A centigrade thermometer gives you a good image for them. I was lucky because my brother and sister are older than I am. When my brother was at the university, I could look at some of his books and learned how to solve a third-degree equation. I was also lucky to meet Mr. Nijs, a high school teacher who, seeing I was interested, gave me very good books to read. I viewed math at that time only as a very nice game. It was a wonderful surprise to learn one could at the same time play and earn one's living.

There is a saying that geometry is the art of thinking correctly with wrong figures. I agree, insisting on the plural. You have more than one picture for each mathematical object. Each of them is wrong but we know how each is wrong. That helps us determine what should be true. It enables you to jump from one setting to another. In mathematics, it is a pleasure when you realize that two things that appear to have nothing in common, in fact, are connected: creating a dictionary between two questions is a powerful tool. Often something will be obvious from one point of view but will give you surprising information if you look at it from another point of view. In mathematics, I have been able to establish such connections a few times.

There are very different ways of thinking within mathematics. Some people are very algebraic, can think with formulae, and are very fast at computing. Some think only in terms of pictures. Some can be extremely precise. Others are very vague and can only give ideas. The diversity is useful because each way of thinking complements the others.

In mathematics, we don't have the enormous collaborations we see in physics or biology with forty participants. I have a number of joint papers, but only one paper with four authors, and we each did something different. Collaboration can take the form of writing a paper together but can also be speaking with people. They can tell you what is obvious for them that was not obvious for you.

I like to be aware of discrepancies or points that I do not understand. I was fortunate to learn quite a lot of algebraic geometry from Alexander Grothendieck and modular forms from others. Mathematicians in those two subjects often did not speak to one another, but I could use an idea of Robert Rankin about modular forms to prove something the algebraic geometers really wanted to know.

In mathematics, there are not only theorems. There are, what we call, "philosophies" or "yogas," which remain vague. Sometimes we can guess the flavor of what should be true but cannot make a precise statement. When I want to understand a problem, I first need to have a panorama of what is around it. A philosophy creates a panorama where you can put the things in place and understand that if you can do something here, you can make progress somewhere else. That is how things begin to fit together.

When I was in Paris as a student, I would go to Grothendieck's seminar at IHES and Jean-Pierre Serre's seminar at the Collège de France. To understand what was being done in each seminar would fill my week. I learned a lot doing so. Grothendieck asked me to write up some of the seminars and gave me his notes. He was extremely generous with his ideas. One could not be lazy or he would reject you. But if you were really interested and doing things he liked, then he helped you a lot. I enjoyed the atmosphere around him very much. He had the main ideas and the aim was to prove theories and understand a sector of mathematics. We did not care much about priority because Grothendieck had the ideas we were working on and priority would have meant nothing. I later met other areas of mathematics where people were worried about doing something first and were hiding what they were doing from one another. I didn't like it. There are all kinds of mathematicians, even competitive ones.

NOAM D. ELKIES

Number theory
Professor of Mathematics, Harvard University

I've played with numbers and music for as long as I can remember—since before age three, according to my parents' records. Music was ubiquitous at home, thanks to my mother's profession as a piano teacher, but she recalls that it was numbers that first piqued my real interest in music. Novices' piano books mark every note 1, 2, 3, 4, or 5 for thumb, index, middle, ring, or little finger, and at first these correspond exactly to notes (because the student's hand does not move), and often also to "scale degrees" (first through fifth notes of the scale) when played by the right hand. For example, the "Ode to Joy" would be 334554321123322 for the right hand, and 332112345543344 for the left, with corresponding digits always adding up to 6. Soon music became a passion in itself, on a par with my passion for numbers, though on its own terms: while music shares some of the tools of basic arithmetic (as with rhythm or harmonics, not just basic fingerings) and the concerns of higher mathematics (such as pattern and economy of means), they serve different ends.

After early tutoring in math from my father (an engineer by profession) and in music from my mother and maternal grandmother, I was fortunate through much of my childhood to have access to wonderful mentors, peers, and other resources in both areas, both in Israel, where I lived from kindergarten through seventh grade, and in New York after we returned. On the math side, these included "math lab" in an enriched grade-school class and a Hebrew introduction to Euclidean geometry during my years in Israel. Back in New York, I read Martin Gardner's *Scientific American* columns and books and participated on Stuyvesant High School's math team, which led to the circuit of local, national, and international high school math contests. I was also introduced, or soon would be introduced, to what would become two of the key themes of my research work to this day: number theory—particularly elliptic curves—and sphere packing in various spaces.

Towards the end of high school, I'd already attained some initial recognition in both mathematics (perfect score in the International Math Olympiad, progress on an open Erdös problem) and music (Juilliard performances and BMI, Broadcast Music Inc., awards for my compositions), but it became clear that I could not aim for careers in both. One reason I chose mathematics was the expectation that I might be able to make my living there and still pursue music at a high level, while the career of a professional musician would likely not allow me to keep up with mathematics except recreationally.

A professional mathematician does original research to create new mathematics. I already had some research experience, but for a long time my best results would not be new: each time, I found that Gauss, perhaps, or Poisson got there first. Later it felt like I was making progress because I was rediscovering theorems dating back only a generation, not a century or two. Even when I at last found a new result in number theory, it was in part because I was unfamiliar with some classic lore: in my doctoral thesis I proved a conjecture on elliptic curves that was thought inaccessible because the standard plan of attack began with proving the generalized Riemann hypothesis! Not knowing this, I tried to better understand why the conjecture might be true and ended up proving it by combining some recently developed number theory with an idea that literally dates back to Euclid.

A few months later I found the first example of a fourth power of a natural number that is the sum of three other such fourth powers, which Euler in 1769 had conjectured is impossible. Even twenty-plus years and dozens of papers later, that remains my best-known result. While others are of greater mathematical consequence, the fourth-power question is one of those problems in number theory that combine an appealingly simple statement with much greater difficulty of solution.

I was fortunate to have solved such a problem, especially so early in my career, and remain fortunate to be able to earn my living at one of my two lifelong passions, thanks in part to that solution. In mathematics as well as music, I have learned much more of the relevant literature and techniques during the intervening years, but even when I use modern tools, it is as a rule not for their own sake but in the service of the traditional concerns and beauties that first drew me to devote so much of my life to the field.

BENEDICT H. GROSS

Number theory
George Vasmer Leverett Professor of Mathematics and former Dean of Harvard College, Harvard University

When I went to college in the '60s, everyone was trying to change the world. Whatever mathematics can do, it's not going to make the world a better place. After graduation, I traveled for several years in Africa, Asia, and Europe, reading mathematics, playing music, and trying to sort this all out. I came to the conclusion that if I wanted to do creative work, it was going to be in mathematics, and returned to the States to study number theory.

In graduate school, I was taught by great mathematicians—John Tate, Jean-Pierre Serre, Raoul Bott, Barry Mazur—and became interested in elliptic curves. An elliptic curve is a cubic equation in two variables. People have studied quadratic equations since the beginning of mathematics; for example, the equation of a circle is $x^2 + y^2 = 1$. A famous elliptic curve studied by Fermat and Euler is $x^3 + y^3 = 1$. Elliptic curves have a richer structure than other equations in two variables, as there is a recipe for producing new solutions from known ones. However, you can have a simple equation which has an infinite number of rational solutions, like $y^2 = x^3 + (1063)^2 x$, where the smallest nonzero solution has over one hundred digits in its numerator and denominator.

As a graduate student, I also met Don Zagier, who was my age but already an established research mathematician. A few years later, I visited Don in Maryland with an idea to show that for certain elliptic curves with rational coefficients, there were an infinite number of solutions—without actually writing any of these rational numbers down. This approach required a bridge between the subject of elliptic curves, which is primarily algebra and geometry, and the subject of modular forms, which is primarily analysis. I would start from one side of the river and Don would start from the other. I sketched this out, and we began to make some preliminary computations.

Towards the end of my visit, we stayed up all night calculating some integrals, making several unrealistic assumptions. After many hours, we arrived at a formula full of nonconvergent infinite sums. Only one term in this expression made any real sense. Don asked me what this term should represent, and I predicted that it would be the power of a prime dividing a singular j-invariant. This seemed implausible—nothing we were doing was even remotely related to j-invariants. Perhaps we were completely lost. Since it was already four o'clock in the morning, I suggested that we go to the library the next day, where there were tables of invariants we could consult. Then I went to sleep.

Don stayed up however, doing computation after computation of j-invariants on his hand computer, checking in each case that the prediction I made was correct. I got up around noon, when Don was sound asleep. The living-room floor was covered with pages and pages of his calculations, each confirming the conjecture. When I got to the last piece of paper it said, "Wake me up immediately!"

That was the high point of my mathematical life. Don and I didn't know if we could establish the final formula, but we knew we had made a good start and were working in completely new territory. It wasn't a crowded field. No one else was looking at this, so there was no rush. Several months later, when we finally got to the end of our individual calculations—his for the derivative of an L-function and mine for the height of a solution—and looked carefully at the many complicated terms, they matched up perfectly. This led to a simple identity, now called the Gross–Zagier formula. No one has really explained why it is true, although Henri Darmon, Steve Kudla, and Shou-Wu Zhang have each made progress in generalizing it.

When you discover a mathematical truth, everything immediately becomes clear. It's so easy to understand. You don't want to touch it. The beauty of mathematics is just a pleasure to behold.

DON ZAGIER

Number theory
Professor of Mathematics, Collège de France, Paris, and Director, Max Planck Institute for Mathematics, Bonn

I moved every year for the first thirty years of my life, so no roots, no stability. In some sense I don't come from anywhere. I grew up in America but have now lived in Europe for so long that I no longer feel very American.

My childhood was unusual. Until age nine, I hardly talked to people and didn't have friends, and I remember nothing of those years. It was thought I might be retarded. The school psychologist gave me a three-hour test and it saved my life. It turned out that I had above average intelligence, and the school said that I could skip a grade if I wanted to. My parents left it up to me to decide. It was the first time I had made any decision about my life. I skipped one grade and then another and another and another, graduating finally from high school at the age of thirteen. After a year in England I went to college at MIT, completing a five-year program in two years, and graduated with two bachelor's degrees at the age of sixteen. I finished my PhD thesis at nineteen. After my fourteenth birthday I never lived with my parents again.

I was both lucky and unlucky in my early mathematical education. Lucky because my father liked math and inspired a love of it in me. We'd walk in the woods and he'd stop in the middle of the walk to show me the Pythagorean theorem and to point to it in nature. He admired mathematics very much and I think it meant a lot to him that I was drawn to it. I was eleven when I decided to be a mathematician. I had a wonderful math teacher who said that special rules would apply to me in class because I wanted to be a professional. So I could read math books during class or work on other problems, but on tests I would receive a zero grade unless everything was perfect. She told me I could choose whether or not I wanted to accept these conditions, and of course I did. It was very good training because I learned to be quick and careful in even routine calculations, and that was very helpful later. But I was also unlucky by starting so young. My high school was in a medium-size town in California, and although I devoured one math book after another, there was no real mathematician to advise me and I chose very old-fashioned books, often more aimed at applied math, that made it hard for me to understand "modern" mathematics later. My first real teacher was in my third year of graduate school, Friedrich Hirzebruch. It was through him that I began to learn to think like a real mathematician. This is something you can't teach yourself but have to learn from a master.

Even now I am not a modern mathematician and very abstract ideas are unnatural for me. I have of course learned how to work with them but haven't really internalized it and remain a concrete mathematician. I like explicit, hands-on formulas. To me they have a beauty of their own. They can be deep or not. As an example, imagine you have a series of numbers such that if you add 1 to any number, you get the product of its left and right neighbors. Then this series will repeat itself at every fifth step! For instance, if you start with 3, 4, then the sequence continues: 3, 4, 5/3, 2/3, 1, 3, 4, 5/3, etc. The difference between a mathematician and a nonmathematician is not just being able to discover something like this, but to care about it and to be curious why it's true, what it means, and what other things in mathematics it might be connected with. In this particular case, the statement itself turns out to be connected with a myriad of deep topics in advanced mathematics: hyperbolic geometry, algebraic K-theory, the Schrödinger equation of quantum mechanics, and certain models in quantum field theory. I find this kind of connection between very elementary and very deep mathematics overwhelmingly beautiful. Some mathematicians find formulas and special cases less interesting and care only about understanding the deep underlying reasons. Of course that is the final goal, but the examples let you see things for a particular problem differently, and anyway it's good to have different approaches and different types of mathematicians.

Mathematics is creative, not a mechanical procedure. It is very personal. Sometimes just from the statement of a result you can guess which mathematician did the work. In some sense, math is already there and true whether we discover it or not—there is a real mathematical world and it is much wider than the physical world of ninety-two elements or sixteen elementary particles. When you find a result, it is not really yours, because it was already true, but you express your personality by the choices you made in discovering and proving it. It's like chess, where the available moves are the same for everybody, but the novice and the expert make very different choices in how to proceed. Except that in chess there are only some twenty moves at any given stage, but in mathematics there are infinitely many. The life of a mathematician is filled with a permanent sense of wonder, and one can never be bored.

BARRY MAZUR

Geometric topology, number theory

Gerhard Gade University Professor, Harvard University

We humans have been taking part in a long conversation—through the millennia—about love, death, how we tell stories about our lives, how we imagine the almost unimaginable, how we have behaved towards one another, how we should behave with each other, and how we think about all this.

That there is a sterling architecture behind how we think, an articulation that transcends mood, circumstance, and even culture, is one of the great gifts of being alive. No mode of thought comes closer to this architecture than mathematics—and this is what makes thinking about mathematics both utterly singular as an experience and universally human.

My current focus in mathematics has to do with numbers; numbers like 1, 2, 3, ... You might already be thinking: given our collective vast understanding of the world, how can there be any issues about something as clear-cut as 1, 2, 3, . . . that are left to be understood?

Yes, this is a conundrum, and possibly somewhere else, on another planet, some alternate intelligence comprehends number as completely as we know our own kitchens, but—despite all of our marvelous present knowledge—we are still at the beginning, and even to achieve what we have up to now, to grasp 1, 2, 3, . . . requires vigorous extension, and full exploitation, of our intuition of the intricacies of geometry and of spaces of many dimensions, of the power of analysis to deal with continuous phenomena, of the subtleties of probability and the laws of chance. That it does so is both one of the great mysteries, and the great glories.

I came to mathematics as, I imagine, many young people did at the time, by being a (very amateurish) radio ham and being perplexed by the incomprehensible power—it seemed—of radio waves, and by contemplating electromagnetic waves and gravity, that weird pair of physical manifestations that each perform the magic trick of action at a distance. I was less interested in what gave rise to gravity and electromagnetic waves (a road that would lead to physics) and more in how in the world one could even formulate the problem of action at a distance, or of phenomena that can only be understood as global and not proximal. The field of topology—which is the first kind of mathematics that I worked in—is a field that has a language that fits this and can deal powerfully with the spaces that it studies, in the large, and with phenomena that cannot be pinned down to any partial vicinity.

Mathematics as an enterprise, too, is best understood "in the large." It has no natural borders, and although I began in topology—and more generally, in various aspects of geometry—the implications of what was being achieved in those fields has broad wings. The intuitions gained from topology can be brought to bear on problems about 1, 2, 3, . . . —and, in fact, for certain problems about number, there is no other effective way of understanding them except via these intuitions, which is what many mathematicians—and I—are currently happily doing.

SIR ANDREW JOHN WILES

Number theory
International Mathematical Union Silver Plaque
Eugene Higgins Professor of Mathematics, Princeton University

When I was ten years old, living in the beautiful university town of Cambridge, England, I had the good fortune one day to stumble across a problem in a book in my local library. On the cover was stated perhaps the most famous of all mathematical problems, at least to the amateur that I then was. It was known as Fermat's Last Theorem and the problem was to show that although it is easy to find many squares of integers which can be written as a sum of two such squares, the same should not be true for cubes, or any higher power. Fermat was an eminent mathematician and he had written this statement in the margin of his copy of a book of Greek mathematics. He claimed that he "truly had a wonderful proof of this theorem but the margin was too small to contain it." Mathematicians ever since had struggled in vain to find a proof. It became my childhood dream to find one.

I passed many hours in attempts to solve this problem. If Fermat had discovered a proof, then his methods would not have been beyond my reach. I continued to think intermittently about Fermat's problem while I was an undergraduate at Oxford, but by the time I started graduate work in number theory, I realized that almost certainly Fermat had been mistaken in his claim and that his methods could not work. So I stopped working on the Fermat equation and started on my career as a professional mathematician. I worked on questions to do with elliptic curves. Although some of these questions go back a thousand years and although the modern study of them began with Fermat, our methods were firmly grounded in the mathematics of the late nineteenth and twentieth centuries.

Then in 1985, a German mathematician, Gerhard Frey, suggested a completely new approach to the Fermat problem. A year later, after work of Jean-Pierre Serre and Kenneth Ribet, the problem of Fermat became inextricably linked to the development of modern mathematics. A completely new approach was possible. Now I had a new opportunity to work on the problem, this time using the theories of elliptic curves and modular forms. The challenge proved irresistible, and for the next eight years I thought about this problem day after day. It was a period of intense work—searching for clues in what had been done, trying and retrying ideas until I could force them to take shape—a period of frustration, too, but punctuated by sudden thrilling insights that encouraged me to think I was on the right track. Then after five years I made a profound discovery. I could reduce the problem to a question that was precisely of the type I had studied in Harvard and during my first years at Princeton, where I had moved permanently in 1982.

During the next two years I worked frantically to try to finish it and in May 1993, I believed I had done so. I presented the results of my work at a conference in Cambridge. At the end of the summer, a problem was pointed out to me that led me to an error in one part of the proof, and I had to set about finding an alternative path for that section. It took me until September of 1994 to find the remedy, during which time I had the assistance of a colleague, Nick Katz, and a former student of mine, Richard Taylor. I will not try to describe the ups and downs of that struggle, the excitements and disappointments, and the ultimate breakthrough in September of 1994 when I finally resolved the last difficulty. But I will say that there is a wonderful magic to fulfilling one's childhood dream. Few perhaps have that privilege and I am fortunate to be one of them.

The year that I spent in correcting the argument was not an easy one. Happily, during 1988, I had married my wife, Nada, and we had two daughters by the time of the Cambridge conference. Our third was born in May of 1994, in time for the final resolution. I cannot imagine that period without the support and demands of a family. It was hard to tear myself away from thinking about the problem every waking moment, but fortunately my daughters managed to distract me just enough to keep some balance in my life. The proof was published in May of 1995 in the *Annals of Mathematics*, some 350 years after Fermat first wrote down the problem.

Mathematics has been studied by mankind for thousands of years. Rulers have come and gone, countries have come and gone, empires have come and gone. But through it all and surviving the wars and the plagues and the famines is the thread of mathematics. It is one of the few constants of human life. The mathematics of the ancient Greeks and Chinese dynasties is as valid now as it was then. Mathematics will continue also into the future. The unsolved problems of today will be the solutions of tomorrow's world. I feel extremely fortunate to be a part of this long and fascinating story.

MANJUL BHARGAVA

Algebra, number theory
Professor of Mathematics, Princeton University

I've always loved mathematics. As a child, I loved shapes and I loved numbers. One of my earliest mathematical memories, from when I was about eight years old, is stacking oranges (which were meant for the family juicer!) in large pyramids. I wanted to know how many oranges would one need to make a triangular pyramid with n oranges on a side? I thought a lot about it, and eventually figured out that the answer is $n(n+1)(n+2)/6$ oranges. That was a very fun and exciting moment for me! I loved that I could predict exactly how many oranges would be needed for any given size of pyramid.

My greatest influences while growing up were my grandfather, a renowned scholar of Sanskrit and ancient Indian history, and my mother, a mathematician with strong interests also in music and linguistics. As a result, I also developed deep interests in language and literature, particularly Sanskrit poetry, and in classical Indian music. I learned to play a number of musical instruments, such as sitar, guitar, violin, and keyboard. But I always enjoyed percussion the most! My favorite instrument was the tabla, a pair of drums, which I started playing as a child and continue to play today, performing whenever I have time.

I always found these three subjects—music, poetry, and mathematics—very similar. This is true, to a large extent, for all pure mathematicians. In school, mathematics is generally grouped in the science category. But for mathematicians, mathematics, like music, poetry, or painting, is a creative art. All these arts involve—and indeed require—a certain creative fire. They all strive to express truths that cannot be expressed in ordinary everyday language. And they all strive towards beauty.

The connection between music/poetry and mathematics is not just an abstract one. While growing up, I learned from my grandfather that incredible mathematics was discovered in ancient times by scholars who did not consider themselves to be mathematicians, but rather poets (or linguists). Linguists such as Panini, Pingala, Hemachandra, and Narayana discovered some wonderful and deep mathematical concepts while studying poetry. The stories that my grandfather told me about them were very inspirational.

There is an example that has been particularly fascinating to me as both a mathematician and a drummer. In the rhythms of Sanskrit poetry, there are two kinds of syllables—long and short. A long syllable lasts two beats, and a short syllable lasts one beat. A question that naturally arose for ancient poets was, how many rhythms can one construct having exactly (say) eight beats, using long and short syllables? (For instance, one might have long-long-long-long, or short-short-short-long-long-short.)

The answer was given in Pingala's classical work Chandashaastra, which dates back to around 500 BC. Here is the elegant solution. We construct a sequence of numbers as follows: First write down the numbers 1 and 2. And then each subsequent number to be written is obtained by adding the two previous numbers. This results in the sequence of numbers 1 2 3 5 8 13 21 34 55 89 . . . . The nth number written tells you the total number of rhythms, consisting of long and short syllables, having n beats. So for eight beats, the answer is that there are thirty-four such rhythms in total.

These numbers are known as the Hemachandra numbers, after the eleventh century linguist who first proved their method of generation. They are also known as the Fibonacci numbers in the West, after the Italian mathematician who wrote about them in the twelfth century. These numbers play an important role now in so many areas of mathematics! They also arise in botany and biology. For example, the number of petals on a daisy always tends to be one of these Hemachandra numbers, as does the number of spirals on a pine cone (for reasons that mathematicians now understand!).

This story inspired me when I was growing up because it is a wonderful example of a simple concept developing into something so omnipresent, important, and deep. In some sense, this is the kind of mathematics that still inspires me today, and that I always strive for, when I do research in number theory. I think the same is true of all mathematicians. It's about finding the simple questions and ideas that lead one to unexpected, unexplored realms—and to deep, elegant, and lasting mathematics.

JOHN T. TATE

Algebraic number theory

Sid W. Richardson Foundation Regents Professor of Mathematics, University of Texas, Austin, and Professor Emeritus, Harvard University

I grew up in Minneapolis as an only child. My father was an experimental physicist at the University of Minnesota. My mother knew the classics and taught high school English until I was born. My father had some books of logic and math puzzles by H. E. Dudeney which fascinated me. Although there were very few I could solve when I was a child, I liked to think about the puzzles.

I would like to express my appreciation of my father. He never pushed me, but from time to time explained some simple fundamental idea, like the fact that the distance a body falls in x seconds is proportional to x^2, or how one can describe points in the plane by coordinates and describe curves by equations. He gave me a very good general idea of what science was about at an early age. I liked math and science but wasn't particularly good at arithmetic and especially hated long division drills.

In high school I read E. T. Bell's book *Men of Mathematics*. Each chapter is a short account of the life and works of a great mathematician. From it I learned of such wonderful things as the quadratic reciprocity law and Dirichlet's theorem on primes in arithmetic progressions. From time to time I tried to imagine how the proofs might go, in vain, of course. I have always preferred to think about something myself than read what others have done. Already as a child with the puzzle books, I didn't like to look at the answers in the back, though I could have learned a lot by doing so. This extreme desire to do things myself has been a strength, but I wish it were complemented by a greater interest and ability in reading works of others. One needs a balance.

Having read in Bell's book about such people as Archimedes, Fermat, Newton, Gauss, Galois, and others, I got the idea that there was no point in being a mathematician if one weren't a genius. I knew I wasn't. I felt that wasn't true of physics because my father was a physicist, so I started graduate school at Princeton in physics. In the first year though, it became clear that math was my true love and best talent, and I was allowed to switch to math.

Princeton would have been an excellent place to do graduate work in math in any case, but it was an especially lucky choice for me because Emil Artin was there. I had never heard of him, and was astonished to learn that he had proved the ultimate generalization of the theorem which interested me most, the quadratic reciprocity law, and that the math book I had most enjoyed reading, Bartel van der Waerden's *Moderne Algebra*, was based on lectures by him and Emmy Noether. Artin was a great mathematician who also loved teaching. He became my mentor and PhD supervisor.

My research has been mainly in number theory and algebraic geometry. Although with the advent of modern computers these subjects have become of great practical importance as the mathematics behind public-key cryptography and the methods of encrypted electronic communication on which modern commerce is based, I did not dream of this as a student, or during most of my life. I loved these subjects for the same reasons they have been studied for centuries: for their own intrinsic interest, for the beauty of the deep relationships which have been discovered and the challenge of finding and proving new ones. It is like a magic book of interrelated puzzles in which the solution to one reveals new pages with several more, and there are no answers in the back. This book was discovered by the ancient Greeks, and their solutions to the first puzzles in it were recorded by Euclid. For example, how to see that the sequence of prime numbers 2, 3, 5, 7, 11, . . . does not end, or that $\sqrt{2}$ is not a rational number. By now we have come far beyond Euclid, and it is next to impossible to describe to a non-mathematician in any but the vaguest terms the solutions we have found and the puzzles we are trying to solve. It is frustrating that mathematics is an art for the initiated. In contrast to music or painting, it is hard to appreciate or enjoy at a popular level without expert knowledge.

Mathematics in itself is a cold subject, completely impersonal, with no connection to people's everyday life and emotions. The warmth in a mathematician's career comes from interactions with colleagues and students, the sharing of ideas, the sense of world-wide community. I greatly appreciate my many mathematical friends for their comradeship and for all I have learned from them.

NICHOLAS MICHAEL KATZ

Number theory, algebraic geometry
Professor of Mathematics, Princeton University

I don't feel very comfortable writing about myself, but around twenty five years ago I was interviewed for what later became the book *Developing Talent in Young People*, which looked at people who had done well in music and art, athletics, or mathematics and science. I will quote myself from the book and comment a bit on what I said then. Actually, the first quote was from my mother, who said, "I have strong feelings about pressuring children and tailoring them to fit parental expectations." This makes me laugh now, because in fact my mother was dead set on my becoming a medical doctor, which my father had been. (He had died when I was two years old, and my mother never remarried.) In order to avoid this fate, I didn't take any biology courses in college, and my refusal to do so led to a tremendous fight with my mother, and to my moving out of her house and moving in with my grandparents (her parents) for my last three years of college.

I talked relatively late and had trouble learning to read. My mother is quoted, "If he hadn't looked so bright, I might have been worried. He was really quite slow. He didn't say his first sentence until he was twenty-four months old." I learned to read in school with a fair amount of difficulty. I think one of the precipitating factors for getting me out of the private school was that it was a progressive school and they didn't actually find out if you knew anything or not. Somehow by the end of the first year, my mother realized that I hadn't learned to read yet. In fact, I was scared of it. In the second grade I happened to have a very warm and sympathetic teacher, and whatever anxiety I had built up about reading, she overcame. Ever since, I have been a big reader, mainly of fiction.

In third grade, a friend and I figured out, the week before we were taught it, how to multiply and divide fractions. And I remember in the fifth grade learning from the encyclopedia the algorithm for doing square roots. And maybe there was only one other kid in the class who knew that. But I didn't have any sense of myself as exceptional or wishing there were other people who could understand what I was thinking about. There were just a few times I remember catching onto things before other people, but I was happy just doing what I was supposed to do. Plane geometry is in some sense the only pure mathematics that anyone has in high school. I wasn't particularly good at it. I wasn't bad at it, but I wasn't crazy about it. For instance, I certainly know mathematicians who discovered all the theorems on their own in high school. I never discovered anything then but I did get good grades.

I got started in mathematics because of one man, Dan Mostow. He and two of his colleagues, Jean-Pierre Meyer and Joe Sampson, had decided that the standard math sequence was terrible. You could not only teach real mathematics to anyone, you should. So with wonderful reformist zeal, they convinced the administration that everyone was going to be in this new course. They were going to teach real mathematics. You were told that you were going to do these good things. I took the course and thought it was terrific. It was obvious to me, and I think to everybody, that I was at least as good as anyone else at Johns Hopkins. There were a few of us who were really good at mathematics. At that time, Ken Ireland was a graduate student, and he was tremendously charismatic and encouraging. In my junior year, I had a course from Bernie Dwork, and the next year I took his graduate course and decided I wanted to work with him. Then he left Hopkins for Princeton and took me with him to be a graduate student there. These three men, Dan Mostow, Ken Ireland, and Bernie Dwork, were the formative influences on me as a student.

It is important to emphasize the incredible role that luck plays in this—having the right professor at the right time, being around when some new mathematical problem is coming into popularity, being exposed to interesting questions. I'm completely convinced that there are lots of mathematicians who are in any measurable way much smarter than I am, higher IQs, they can learn more, they can learn faster, answer questions more quickly. I'm a much better mathematician in the sense that I've done better mathematics, and this is very largely a question of luck, of being in the right place at the right time. You have to be pretty good at mathematics, but if you are pretty good at mathematics and around people who are interested in uninteresting mathematics, you'll be pretty good at uninteresting mathematics.

Some of these remarks were published in *Developing Talent in Young People*, Benjamin S. Bloom, editor, Ballantine Books, New York, 1985.

KENNETH RIBET

Algebraic number theory, algebraic geometry
Professor of Mathematics, University of California, Berkeley

My father is a certified public accountant. In the days before calculators and spreadsheets, he often spent hours at the dining table adding long columns of numbers. My dad taught me addition (with carrying) when I was a small boy. Not long after, I learned from him the secrets of subtraction, fractions, and decimals. Perhaps this is the reason that I became fascinated by numbers as a child. In any case, I was delighted to be able to do arithmetic operations long before they were introduced in school. When I was a bit older, I spent hours with a mathematics review book that I found with my parents' college textbooks. I struggled to learn the concepts in that book and felt a great sense of accomplishment at the end of each chapter.

Right through high school, math was my best and my favorite subject. I joined the math team in seventh grade and became captain of my high school math team when I was a senior. I liked puzzles and problems, but I was never a real whiz at them. One boy who was a grade ahead of me, Stanley Rabinowitz, was an absolute ace at problems of all kinds. He taught me arcane theorems in plane geometry that I used as secret weapons in math competitions. As an adult, Stan founded MathPro Press, a publishing company that specializes in mathematics problem books.

After my junior year in high school, I spent the summer in a science program on the campus of Brown University. I learned calculus from an engineering professor and fell in love with Brown. I studied calculus again as a high school senior and felt a great sense of mastery toward the end of the year when I understood the epsilon-delta arguments that our textbook presented. After I was accepted at Brown, Professor Frank M. Stewart mailed me a set of problems that served as a written entrance exam for his honors sophomore-level course. My familiarity with epsilons and deltas enabled me to make the cut.

The day that I walked into Frank Stewart's class, I got hooked on abstract mathematics. I had come to Brown with only the vaguest idea of what it meant to be a university professor. I liked my math professors, and I wanted to be exactly like them. During my time at Brown, I was mentored by two exceptional individuals: Mike Rosen and Kenneth Ireland. Ireland was happy to give me lots of directives: he told me exactly what I should be reading (articles by André Weil) and where I should be headed ("Go to Harvard and work with Tate").

I did go to Harvard, and I did work with John Tate. As a Harvard graduate student, I learned the subject of arithmetic geometry, and I haven't looked back. First as a student and then as a working mathematician, I have been the lucky beneficiary of the insights and guidance of some of the giants of the subject. You will find portraits of these giants elsewhere in this book.

PERSI WARREN DIACONIS

Probability, statistics; magician

Mary V. Sunseri Professor of Statistics and Mathematics, Stanford University

I was born into a family of professional musicians and I studied violin for nine years. I finished high school early and entered the City College of New York when I was fourteen. Shortly after this, Dai Vernon, who was the greatest magician in the United States at the time, invited me to go on tour with him. I left home without even telling my parents and began a very interesting life. I loved doing magic and was very good at it. I enjoyed inventing new tricks and teaching others to do them. After about eight years, a friend recommended a book on probability by William Feller. I couldn't understand it so decided to go back to school. Less than three years later, I graduated with a degree in math and was accepted into the statistics program at Harvard. By 1974, I had earned my PhD and was on the statistics faculty at Stanford University.

I still love magic, but what makes me happiest is a beautiful mathematical idea meeting a real-world problem so that both are illuminated. For example, the real-world problem, how many times should a deck of cards be shuffled to mix it up? connects to the esoteric corners of a noncommutative Fourier analysis. I learned Fourier analysis because I wanted to understand shuffling. Dave Bayer and I showed that, for ordinary riffle shuffling of fifty-two card decks, seven shuffles are necessary and suffice. Changing the shuffle under study calls for new group theory. The new group theory turns out to be useful in a chemistry problem, and so it goes.

Every once in a while, crude tools get honed and improved, collections of disparate problems coalesce, theory is called for and developed, and a little field is born. My work on "exchangeability" with David Freedman has this flavor. This starts out as a philosophy problem (what do we mean when we say an event has probability 1/3?). Following in the footsteps of the Italian philosopher-mathematician Bruno de Finetti, many special cases were carefully worked out. Tiring of proving the same kind of result over and over, an abstract (and close to un-understandable) general theory was worked out. I'm not proud of the abstraction, but it's part of being a professional.

One difference between my statistical persona and my mathematical persona is that I want to see things carried through to concrete applications. After developing the theory behind a cryptography chip, it's a true thrill to see thousands of them coming off a production line and being inserted into TV sets.

I've had the luck to be connected to great universities (mostly Stanford and Harvard). Students can ask "silly" questions that turn my head around. When I review the areas I work in—rates of convergence for Markov chains (a fancy version of card shuffling), exchangeability, probabilistic number theory—I'm astounded at how much of the work I'm known for was actually carried out by my students (and their students, and so on). It's sometimes frustrating. I write now from a conference where great-grandstudents have presented ideas I invented without mentioning where they came from.

Right now, I'm alarmed by a drastic change in one of my worlds: the magician side of me has kept secrets for all of my life. Many of these secrets are now permanently on display for anyone via the Internet. Because of this, other secrets are tumbling out of notebooks into the public eye. An essential ingredient of the magician's trade is truly and permanently lost. Perhaps the sheer mass of exposure will protect the gems scattered within. Perhaps the exposure will make an educated public appreciate the difference between the shrill huckster and the practiced artist. Most probably, the secret world I spent my life in is just gone.

I'm contributing to the mess, finishing a book with the mathematician-juggler Ron Graham. We get around some problems of exposure by using tricks that we've invented. The tricks we explain also have a real mathematical component. I find it wonderful that simple questions about shuffling cards can lead beyond what two thousand years of mathematics can answer.

PAUL MALLIAVIN

Probability, harmonic analysis

Professor Emeritus of Mathematics, University of Paris VI: Pierre et Marie Curie

I was born into a family of intellectuals who were deeply involved in politics for several generations, either by writing books or by exercising political responsibilities at a national level in France. I have the highest respect for the fighting life of my parents, uncles, and grandparents; I have often seen their disillusions after fighting for carefully planned political proposals that were finally withdrawn. One of my reasons for choosing mathematics has been that as soon as truth is discovered, it enters immediately into reality.

I finished my graduate studies in mathematics at the Sorbonne in Paris in 1946. I had the good fortune of taking graduate courses taught by great masters of the French school from the beginning of the twentieth century: Émile Borel for integration and Élie Cartan for geometry. A new "French Revolution" rose in Paris in 1947. It was driven by Henri Cartan and Jean Leray. I also owe a special debt to Szolem Mandelbrojt, with whom I wrote my thesis.

Marston Morse and Arne Beurling invited me to the Institute for Advanced Study for several years (1954–1955 and 1960–1961). My sojourn there was an invaluable opportunity to establish long-lived interactions with mathematicians firstly from Princeton and also from Chicago, MIT, Stanford, and New York, followed by mathematicians from Barcelona, Stockholm, Moscow, Lisbon, Kyoto, Wuhan, Pisa, and Bonn. These interactions led me to be one of the founders of the *Journal of Functional Analysis*, which has now just published its 252nd volume.

I am fully convinced of the fundamental unity of mathematics, which I thought I could serve by establishing relations between fields that seemed relatively unrelated. In 1954, I solved a problem on Fourier series by developing a symbolic functional calculus on distributions; in 1972 I started a new field, stochastic differential geometry, by mixing Élie Cartan's geometry with Kiyoshi Itō's theory of stochastic processes; in 1978 I began another new field, the stochastic calculus of variations; in 2001, under the impulse of Pierre-Louis Lions, I developed stochastic calculus of variations in the context of mathematical finance; last year I worked on classical Euler equations of deterministic incompressible fluid dynamics by using tools of stochastic differential geometry.

My mathematical wandering was made possible by my appointment as a full professor at the age of thirty, which enabled me to continue my career with relative freedom. A difficulty in this wandering is how to be considered a colleague rather than a strange amateur when entering a new field, one whose publications have to be taken seriously. In this connection, I owe a great debt to Daniel W. Stroock, who in his extensive work supported my stochastic calculus of variations, for which he coined the name, Malliavin calculus. Finally, I have always taken the greatest care to keep my scientific activities independent of any political or geographical considerations, feeling that mathematics is a universal truth.

WILLIAM ALFRED MASSEY

Applied probability, stochastic processes, queueing theory
Edwin S. Wilsey Professor of Operations Research and Financial Engineering, Princeton University

My parents, Juliette and Richard Massey Sr., were both educators; she was from Chattanooga, Tennessee, and he was from Charlotte, North Carolina. They met at Lincoln University in Jefferson City, Missouri, which became my birthplace. My initial fascination with numbers started when my mother would let me play with plastic numbers and cut-up old calendars.

We moved to Saint Louis, Missouri, when I was four. There I came of age educationally during the post-Sputnik era. A fifth-grade gifted program exposed me to Euclidean geometry and number systems of differing bases. My interest in drawing and graphic arts helped me to appreciate the uses of perspective and proportion. It was exciting to discover that only a ruler and compass were needed to draw a regular hexagon. In seventh grade, I was given an exam involving the type of abstract reasoning that I would later see in a high school algebra course. Not only did I excel on this test but also scored well beyond everybody else in the class. This is when I knew that I wanted to become a mathematician. Starting high school in the Saint Louis suburb of University City, I learned about trigonometry, vectors with dot and cross products, as well as single and multivariable calculus with divergences and curls. This knowledge was supplemented by a growing appreciation of the critical role that mathematical concepts were playing in my chemistry and physics classes.

My true understanding of mathematics as a researcher began as a college student at Princeton University. I specialized in abstract algebra and number theory while mastering real, complex, and functional analysis. I also maintained my scientific interests by taking physics courses all four years. Upon graduating magna cum laude, I was awarded a competitive Bell Laboratories fellowship that was established to increase the number of minority PhD's in the sciences. It paid for my pursuit of the doctorate of philosophy in mathematics at Stanford University.

The summers spent as a graduate student at Bell Laboratories exposed me to the world of applied mathematics and gave me my first research publication in 1978. It was here that I developed an interest in queueing theory. This is a branch of applied probability that was invented for the design and performance analysis of telephone systems. The resulting mathematics produces theorems, formulas, and algorithmic tools that assist communication engineers and business managers in making strategic, data-driven decisions. This interest in the mathematics of communications led me to work full time as a member of technical staff in the Mathematical Sciences Research Center at Bell Laboratories after obtaining my PhD from Stanford in 1981.

I was doubly fortunate to have worked at Bell Labs. It was the leading center of industrial research in communications. Moreover, Bell Labs during the last three decades of the twentieth century had a critical mass of African-American researchers. This created for the minority scientists and engineers working there a sense of purpose and professional accomplishment similar to what the Harlem Renaissance was for African-American artists and poets. Upon leaving the labs in 2001, I accepted a position at Princeton University as the Edwin S. Wilsey Professor in the Department of Operations Research and Financial Engineering.

I have made many original contributions as a mathematician by developing a theory of dynamical queueing systems. Classical queueing models assumed that calling rates were constant, so they could use the static, equilibrium analysis of time-homogeneous Markov chains. However, real communication systems call for the large-scale analysis of queueing models with time-varying rates. My thesis at Stanford University created a dynamic, asymptotic method for time-inhomogeneous Markov chains called "uniform acceleration" to deal with such problems. Moreover, my research on queueing networks led to new methods of comparing multidimensional, Markov processes by viewing them as stochastic orderings on partially ordered spaces. Finally, one of my most cited papers develops an algorithm to find a dynamic, optimal server staffing schedule for telephone call centers with time-varying demand, which led to a patent. Another highly cited paper creates a temporally and spatially dynamic model for the offered load traffic of wireless communication networks.

HAROLD WILLIAM KUHN

Game theory, mathematical economics
Professor Emeritus of Mathematical Economics, Princeton University

The longer I live, the more I believe that our lives are controlled by chance events and the actions of others. My own life confirms this thesis. Here is a chronological account.

My life in mathematics may well have been begun by my electric shop teacher, Mr. Brockway, at James A. Foshay Junior High School in South Central Los Angeles. When I was eleven years old, he taught me the miracle of logarithms and set me to solving problems of arranging switches (single- and double-pole) to control lights in complex ways. These "puzzles" were intrinsically combinatorial problems of the sort that have played a central role in all of my research. Mr. Brockway, who moonlighted by providing the movie studios of Hollywood with high-fidelity, long-playing, audio equipment, left me with the ambition to be a radio engineer.

At Manual Arts High School, we benefited from the fact that, during the depression, teaching was a steady job; consequently, we had high school teachers with PhD's in chemistry and physics. It was my physics teacher, Mr. Paden, who took me to a science fair at Caltech, and planted in my mind the idea of going to Caltech to become an electrical engineer. My fallback school was UCLA, which admitted anyone with a B average in a California high school. UCLA had the disadvantage of requiring, as a land-grant college, participation in ROTC, an anathema to me.

And so I was one of 160 freshman at Caltech in the fall of 1942, the only freshman to live off campus. The reason was simple: my parents were too poor to afford the room and board costs at Caltech, so they moved to Pasadena and rented a house near the campus for $25 a month. My father had suffered a severe heart attack in 1939, and the entire family income was about $1,200 a year from a disability insurance policy. Neither of my parents had gone to school beyond the fifth grade, so my scholastic ambitions were something of a mystery to them. At Caltech, I morphed from an electrical engineer into a double major in mathematics and physics, when I was drafted into the army in July 1944, in the middle of my junior year.

After finishing basic training in the infantry, I qualified for the Army Specialized Training Program in Japanese and was sent to Yale University. E. T. Bell, with whom I had taken several courses, gave me an introduction to Øystein Ore, who allowed me to audit his graduate course in abstract algebra. In the same period, a friend from Caltech, Earnie Rauch, had been drafted with me, then discharged for medical reasons, and had transferred to Princeton University to finish his undergraduate degree in mathematics. I wangled a several-day leave from Yale to visit him and so sat in on classes given by Emil Artin, Claude Chevalley, and Salomon Bochner, which left me convinced that Princeton was the place to go for graduate study in mathematics.

Discharged from the army in 1946, I returned to Caltech to finish my undergraduate studies in June 1947. By then I was clear in my mind that mathematics was my calling. My feeling was strengthened by the presence at Caltech of Frederic Bohnenblust, who had been brought to Princeton by Hermann Weyl. Bohnenblust brought a breath of fresh air to the mathematics at Caltech, supplying a modern point of view to a department that had been stuck in turn-of-the-century, English-style analysis. He also supported my application to Princeton, walking to my house one weekend (we were too poor to have a telephone) to invite me to his house to meet Solomon Lefschetz, who was chair of the mathematics department at the time.

Thus, by this circuitous and chance-laden route, I was led to my real training as a mathematician. But, there was one more time when chance would play a role in shaping my career. While starting a thesis on group theory with Ralph Fox, using topological methods to prove algebraic results, I joined Al Tucker and a fellow graduate student, David Gale, in a summer project to study the relationship between the just-born subjects of game theory and linear programming. This project set the course of my subsequent academic career, which has centered around the applications of mathematics to economics.

Every mathematician has "favorite children." Mine are my formulation of extensive games as trees, the Hungarian method, and pivoting methods for approximating fixed points and providing an elementary proof of the fundamental theorem of algebra. These are all combinatorial problems and thus belong to the same family as the switching problems that were posed to me as an eleven-year-old.

AVI WIGDERSON

Theoretical computer science, complexity, cryptography
Professor of Mathematics, Institute for Advanced Study, Princeton

I grew up in Haifa, Israel, in a tiny apartment overlooking the Mediterranean. My father was an engineer who loved math. He was very interested in teaching me and my two brothers, but I was more inclined than my siblings. We spent lots of time solving problems and puzzles from old Russian books that he brought with him to Israel after the Second World War.

In school I enjoyed learning everything, but mathematics in particular, from very early on. After my army service, I chose computer science as my major at the Technion. It may have been more natural to choose math, but my parents thought it would be a good idea to study something that had prospects of a real job. I didn't think of an academic career then. I grew up in a blue-collar neighborhood and I didn't know any academics as a kid.

Luckily, the computer science major included, beyond programming and systems courses, plenty of math and theory of computer science courses, which I loved. Like most top students of my class, I applied to PhD programs in the United States. I got into Princeton as a graduate student in computer science. Only then did the concepts of research and an academic career become clear, and extremely attractive. I knew that this was what I wanted to do with my life.

In theoretical computer science I have found a perfect research area. It is mathematics, but an extremely young branch of it, only a few decades old. It is full of excitement, many basic unsolved problems, and many young, talented, and enthusiastic researchers. Even more, new questions keep arising externally, from new technologies requiring modeling and from computational challenges in need of efficient solutions.

To get a glimpse of the type of problems which occupy me and my colleagues, you only have to wonder how your computer or your body (especially your brain), performs difficult tasks so efficiently. On the computer side—how does MapQuest find a route between two points so quickly? How does Google locate the needle you look for in a huge information stack in a blink? and so on. Fast hardware is usually only a small part of the answer. The bigger part is the extremely clever algorithms developed for such problems by computer scientists. And on the human side—how do our bodies fight disease, fold proteins, recognize faces, memorize text? Here algorithms were discovered by nature over billions of years of evolution, and scientists attempt to first model the computational platform and then reverse-engineer these clever algorithms.

An even bigger challenge than finding efficient algorithms for important problems, is proving that for other important problems such algorithms do not exist (namely proving that these problems are inherently intractable). This challenge has not yet been met in full generality. But despite natural reaction, proving that a given problem is hard is not necessarily bad news. Computer scientists have found ingenious ways of utilizing hard problems, for example, for computer security. Almost all electronic commerce today is based on the assumed difficulty of a single computational problem. But is it really hard?

Computational thinking is essential to scientific theories of biology and physics and also to basic issues such as privacy, learning, randomness, and more. The intellectual challenges in understanding these, and computation itself, will occupy us for many years. Working in a dynamic mathematical area of such depth, beauty, and importance is an unending source of joy for me.

ARLIE PETTERS

Mathematical physics: light and gravity
Professor of Mathematics and Physics, Duke University

Imagine majestic night skies filled with sparkling points of starlight scattered like diamonds across the heavens. These were the evening visual experiences of my childhood in the tiny Central American town of Dangriga, Belize. I constantly asked questions about the universe, often times causing my elders to worry about my obsession: Does space continue forever? How did the universe come about? Why do we exist? Is there a God? This early exposure to the profound beauty and mystery of the cosmos has since gripped and steered my intellectual journey.

At fourteen years, I immigrated to the United States. I attended Canarsie High School in Brooklyn for two years and proceeded to Hunter College of the City University of New York with the objective of studying Einstein's theory. At Hunter I was in an accelerated five-year BA-MA program in mathematics for exceptional undergraduates, while I also majored in physics with a minor in philosophy. My first year of college was marked by personal hardships, which were resolved when Professor Jim Wyche rescued me with a Minority Access to Research Careers Fellowship. Though my remaining college years were consumed with laying a solid foundation in general relativity, I did find time to lift weights, dance, date, and interact with students of all races and from widely diverse international backgrounds. This experience was a personal cultural melting pot!

After Hunter, I pursued a PhD at MIT with a concentration in mathematical physics. My studies were sponsored by a Bell Labs Cooperative Research Fellowship for underrepresented minority students. My graduate school years were actually split between MIT and Princeton under two thesis advisors, Professors Bertram Kostant (mathematician, MIT) and David Spergel (astrophysicist, Princeton).

From the time I entered graduate school, I mapped out in detail the mathematics and physics tools I wanted to master during the first two years. I worked relentlessly to develop the ability to move freely between mathematical and physical insights, leveraging the benefits of rigorous and heuristic arguments; navigate through dense forests of lengthy, technical calculations, while utilizing analytics and software technology; carry out highly abstract mathematical reasoning that may unveil surprising logical truths with universal reach; and discern when a mathematical theorem is beautiful, when it is in natural aesthetic balance.

I received my PhD from MIT in 1991 and taught at MIT for two years. I was an assistant professor at Princeton for five years and then proceeded to Duke in 1998, where I am presently a professor of mathematics and physics. Along the way, I have received numerous awards and honors, for which I am thankful. These achievements have helped me inspire many young people in the United States and Belize to pursue mathematics and science careers.

I study how gravity acts on light, an effect known as gravitational lensing that was considered by Einstein. I have studied the effect on light produced by passing a number of stars, the cosmic shadows cast in the universe by gravitational fields, the strong deflection of light by black holes, the possibility of an extra dimension to the universe, and most recently some problems connected with the cosmic censorship conjecture, dealing with the issues arising when examining singularities at which current physics falls apart. I enjoy interdisciplinary work, particularly the synergies among mathematics, astronomy, and physics created by the study of light and gravity.

Let me close by commenting on a question I am often asked and which brings me back to the beginning of the essay: do you believe in God? God, love, meditation, and prayer are an integral part of my day-to-day life. The scientific method is a powerful tool that I also integrate nondogmatically into my worldview. Like any instrument, this method has its limitations; it is designed to address the question "how?" rather than "why?" and even in the domain of "how?" it is not all-seeing. So, as important as it is, the scientific method has practical relevance only to a restricted part of the human condition. Indeed, the moment I begin to act as if science can access and resolve all the deep mysteries of existence, pinch me! And as I awaken, lovingly and forgivingly remind me that I am only human.

INGRID CHANTAL DAUBECHIES

Applied mathematics, wavelets
William R. Kenan, Jr., Professor of Mathematics and Applied and Computational Mathematics, Princeton University

I was born and grew up in the coal-mine region in Belgium. I studied theoretical physics, so I don't have a single math degree. I started my research work on mathematical physics, which is basically mathematics focused on or motivated by physics. A few years after my PhD, I became interested in applying mathematics not only to understanding the physical world around us, but also to technology, where you construct things. The mathematical analysis may also lead you to construct things differently, rather than study the already existing world.

Something funny struck me after I made that transition. I had contributed to building wavelet bases—new tools to analyze digital signals and images—and I realized that everyone considered the new mathematical concepts associated with those as "constructed," that is, built by the mathematicians who first published them. That is different from the way most (pure) mathematicians consider their work: they feel more like discoverers, who uncover new territory; they feel strongly that "it" is already there, and they just discover it. This realization made me think—I knew exactly what the more "pure" mathematicians meant, because I had felt it myself: the sense of wonder at finally understanding the full structure that explains many earlier observations. I had felt it in work that I had done before, where many other mathematicians would have agreed that the work was one of "discovery." Working on wavelets had felt exactly the same—yet, here most mathematicians viewed it as "construction" rather than discovery. This puzzle made me want to find the boundary between these two mathematical realms. I haven't found it and I am now convinced that it doesn't exist: all our mathematics is constructed. It is a construction we make in order to think about the world. I would even go so far as to say that mathematical thinking is the *only* way we have to think logically about things we observe. There are other ways in which we experience the world and in which we interact with it—ways that have to do more with emotions and sensual delight and that lead to other wonderful things, like love and art—but when we want to think logically, we basically are back to what is essentially mathematics. So I don't quite agree with Galileo: the book of Nature is not written in mathematics; rather, mathematics is the only language *we* know to explain nature logically. We like logical thinking as an activity—figuring out things gives us pleasure. That is why mathematical puzzles like Sudoku or Rubik's Cube have become so popular. This doesn't mean that everyone is equally likely to enjoy highly advanced mathematics—liking mathematics and being good at it to the point of becoming a professional mathematician is a bit like becoming a professional athlete—but it does mean you don't have to have a weird talent to "get" mathematics, just as you can enjoy sport and exercise even if it isn't your profession.

Many of the problems on which I have been working exploit in some way the idea that the object or solution we are looking for has a "sparse" description. What that means is that you have a collection of questions you can ask about the object, and you know that there is some way to completely determine the identity of the unknown object by obtaining the answers to just a few (say ten) questions, but they have to be the "right" ten questions. You have no idea ahead of time which questions will be right for this particular query—it could be any small collection of them. One problem is then whether you can pick a set of say twenty *fixed* questions ahead of time so that from their answers you will always be able to get a precise description of an *arbitrary* unknown sparse object, regardless of what the right ten questions were for that particular object. Computer scientists have known for a while how to solve some problems of this type, and their insights are used for example in the design of algorithms for Internet search engines. Now that technology has advanced to the point where we can collect more measurement results than we can handle, different questions of a similar type come up in many other fields. For the moment three collaborations in which my students and I participate, in the completely different fields of geophysics, biology, and neuroscience, all have turned up sparsity problems of this type. It is important to develop algorithms that can deal with these new problems and that can do it fast. To prove convergence of these algorithms for almost all possible solutions in which you might be interested, the mathematical fields that come into play are quite different from those traditionally used in applied mathematics, so I have to learn whole new ways of thinking. That is one thing I like a lot about applied mathematics: to some extent, the problem dictates what mathematical subfields you have to learn, and so you often have to learn new material. And that is what I enjoy: learning to bend my mind around new obstacles, learning to master new patterns.

SIR ROGER PENROSE

Mathematical physics, geometry
Rouse Ball Professor Emeritus of Mathematics, University of Oxford

My original feelings for mathematics were very much stimulated by my father, Lionel Penrose, a physician who specialized in the inheritance of mental disorders, later becoming professor of human genetics at University College London. He was a multitalented man of Quaker background, his father having been a professional artist. He much enjoyed puzzles, chess, painting, music, biology, astronomy, and mathematics. I recall many walks in the country with him, my mother, and my two brothers—and much later my young sister also—which gave him opportunities to explain things about nature.

Both of my brothers were expert chess players (my younger brother Jonathan was British chess champion a record ten times). Several walks with my father and brothers, with one brother far out in front and the other far behind and my father in the middle, found the three of them playing Kriegspiel in their heads, a form of chess where two opponents (in this case my brothers) knew just the locations of their own pieces, and they had to infer from the legality of their attempted moves where the opponent's pieces might be. Only the umpire (here my father) knew the entire position. My job was just to be the runner, conveying the (suggested) moves from brother to father and back again—not serious mental activity, but good exercise!

Although needing mathematics (largely statistics) for his work, it was my father's *enjoyment* of the subject that made a strong impression on me. At quite a young age (around ten) I learned from him about regular and semi-regular polyhedra, and we made many models. One event struck me particularly when I was about sixteen. I told my father that my mathematics schoolteacher was to start on calculus the following day. Seeming somewhat alarmed, my father immediately took me aside and expertly demonstrated the essentials and elegance of the calculus. I think that what impressed me most was his desire to be the one to reveal to me the subject's deep beauty, and I realized how precious the subject of mathematics is. Ironically, when I later decided to study mathematics (at University College London) he was initially against this choice, as he viewed a career in this subject as appropriate only for those without skills in any other scientific area!

Afterwards, I went to Cambridge to do a PhD in pure mathematics (algebraic geometry), but there I was inspired by lectures by Hermann Bondi on general relativity and cosmology, by Paul Dirac on quantum theory, and by the warm friendship of Dennis Sciama to move into theoretical physics. The breadth of influences that I encountered at Cambridge, together with a lifelong input from my father and my older brother Oliver, helped me to develop a perhaps rather individualistic approach to basic questions in physics. I was especially attracted to Einstein's curved spacetime theory of general relativity, and I innovated geometric techniques to demonstrate the inevitability of singularities (situations so extreme that current physics "gives up") inside what we now refer to as "black holes." These techniques were subsequently adopted by Stephen Hawking.

Geometrical ideas were central to my introduction of the theory of twistors, which analyzes spacetime and quantum physics from an unusual perspective. They have also been central to some of my later proposals with regard to cosmology.

Drawing pictures has always been important for me, both in research and exposition. This helped me to develop sets of geometrical shapes (sometimes referred to as "Penrose tiles") that tile the entire plane without repetition like the figure below.

ROBERT ENDRE TARJAN

Theoretical computer science

James S. McDonnell Distinguished University Professor of Computer Science, Princeton University, and Senior Fellow, HP Labs

I was born in 1948 in Pomona, California. My father was the director of a state hospital for the developmentally disabled, and I lived on the grounds of the hospital until I went to college. The patients were very nice, but the kids at school teased me because I was smart but living in a place where others were not so smart. Through reading science fiction as a child, I became interested in science, specifically astronomy. My goal was to be the first person on Mars. In the seventh grade, I read some of Martin Gardner's articles on mathematical games in *Scientific American*. His articles inspired many kids, including me, to become interested in mathematics. I had a remarkable eighth-and-ninth-grade math teacher in public school, who was doing his own flavor of new math before it became popular (and then unpopular). He taught us formal mathematics, including axioms and proofs, which I found very exciting.

As a high school student, I was in a summer science program in which we calculated asteroid orbits. It gave me some exposure to computers, which I also got while working in the research lab at the state hospital. Computers were the size of refrigerators and were programmed using punched paper tape or punch cards. My first exposure to programming was assembly language. FORTRAN, an early high-level computer language, was a revelation. Unfortunately we had to do our orbit calculations on mechanical calculators the size of typewriters, one painful operation at a time.

I went to Caltech as an undergraduate and majored in math. I applied to different graduate schools in computer science and in math and ended up going to Stanford to get a PhD in computer science. I planned to study artificial intelligence but instead did research on the design and analysis of combinatorial algorithms. I've been working in this area ever since.

The goal of my work is to devise step-by-step recipes (algorithms) for solving various computational problems on a computer. The problems I study do not involve numbers as much as they involve patterns or arrangements of the input data. An example is the problem of finding a shortest path from point A to point B in a road network. The structure of the road network is the most important part of the problem: the length of a path is just the sum of the lengths of the road segments making up the path. One way to solve such a problem is to list all possible paths and choose the shortest. But for a road network of any size, there are too many possible paths, and this method is infeasible for even the fastest computers. An alternative, much faster method is to explore the network greedily, starting from point A and always proceeding to the next point closest to A, until eventually reaching B. Making such a search efficient requires keeping track of the points already reached, the neighboring points, and their distances. A colleague and I developed an especially efficient way of doing this.

To solve problems like this one requires a combination of the right algorithm design and careful structuring of the data: the information needed to solve the problem must be stored on a computer so that it is easy to access and also easy to update as the solution process unfolds. Different problems have different data-structuring requirements, but research over the last fifty years or so by many people has revealed common themes among problems and has produced a rich understanding of the landscape of algorithm design and data structuring. The analysis of algorithm performance has become very sophisticated and uses tools from many branches of mathematics. In spite of all this progress, the field of algorithm design and analysis continues to be exciting. I do not foresee any shortage of interesting problems any time soon.

I now split my time between Princeton University and Hewlett-Packard. This gives me the chance to leaven the ivory tower of academia with a dose of reality. The university gives me the opportunity to work with bright, eager young people, to convey to them the sheer beauty of my field, and to share with them the thrill of discovery. On the other hand, industrial research offers the chance to move my ideas into the real world—to find out what methods are useful in practice and how theory needs to be changed to better match practice. Industry is also a rich source of new problems to solve. My goal is always to develop methods justified by theory and simple and efficient in practice—in short, elegant algorithms.

DAVID HAROLD BLACKWELL

Mathematical statistics

Professor Emeritus of Mathematics, University of California, Berkeley

I grew up in Illinois in a town called Centralia, whose main industries were railroading and coal mining. All Blacks in Centralia came in 1912 or 1919 as strikebreakers for the Illinois Central Railroad. My father worked for the railroad, and I grew up with an antiunion bias because that was what had gotten my father a job in the first place.

I was always the smartest boy in my class although there were always three or four girls ahead of me. Math was the only subject in which I was the best of all the students. I especially liked geometry in high school. The idea of picking one triangle (these were just imaginary triangles) and putting it on another one to see how they fit: that was beautiful stuff. It was very different from anything else I had encountered. In mathematics, one discovers things that are true but not obvious.

Grown people liked to come around, pat me on the head, and ask what I was going to be when I grew up. I found that if I told them I was going to be a teacher, they accepted that response and went away happy. I started believing it myself, especially when a friend of my father's said he would give me a teaching job after I finished college. That settled it because it was in the 1920s and early '30s. Getting a job was very important. I was going to be an elementary school teacher. At the University of Illinois, I majored in mathematics and decided I'd like to be a high school math teacher instead. I kept adjusting my ideas as I continued in school and finally decided to be a college math teacher. After graduation, I thought with some correctness that my only opportunity would be in Black schools. There were 105 Black colleges in 1941. I wrote 105 letters of application and got three offers. I didn't look outside Black schools and that's the main way being Black made a difference. My first three jobs were at Black colleges. Then I came to Berkeley and have been here ever since. I've enjoyed teaching very much.

I have also done quite a bit of research. It was not my intention to do research. I started out to learn and liked understanding what other people had done. But, sometimes in trying to understand what other people have done, you get a different slant on something and a question they hadn't answered occurs to you. You pursue it. I've written and published about eighty research papers. I thought each one had a different origin and focus, although all but about six of those papers are about probability.

I was retired from teaching at age seventy. If I'd been free to continue, I would have and that would have been a mistake. My ability to think and my energy were declining. It's good to recognize when it's time to move on. I came across one of my old papers the other day and I could barely understand it. I thought, "Wow, this guy is good! How could he think of that?" The mind changes. When I look at what I've done, I'm impressed. I've been very lucky.

AFTERWORD BRANDON FRADD

This book came about because I had the wonderful opportunity to meet Mariana Cook and her husband Hans Kraus. We hit it off! Mariana sent me a book of photographs of famous scientists she had published and I immediately asked if she would do one of mathematicians. She loved the idea!

Great mathematicians have usually been considered rather different from the rest of the population, but of course they are people just like everyone else. I think that to be great at mathematics, you probably do have to have some differences: an ability to concentrate in a certain way, detach from the distractions of the environment around you, and envision possibilities that others might label "crazy." Still, they are regular people, too, who marry, form clubs, vote, and push their kids on swing sets. How different are they? How could we even tell? This beautiful book answers some of these questions. In these portraits, you will see how similar mathematicians are to us and how they are different from one another. You will have a glimpse of each personality through the expressions and the poses. The photographs along with the essays will give you an idea of the unique qualities of each individual. The essays have been carefully written either by the mathematician or Mariana Cook, based on personal conversations she had with them. They are all different and each captures something special.

There are many reasons why I asked Mariana to take these photographs. I have always loved math. I love figuring out a problem. Actually, the problem grabs me and I can't get away from it. I am obsessed by the problem until I figure out the solution. I love seeing relations among things. I can't help it. It just seems to be who I am. I always knew I would major in mathematics in college. I started first at Columbia and then finished at Princeton where there were many legendary people, and lots of "can you believe this?" stories. Burt Totaro was the youngest student admitted as an undergraduate to Princeton and John Milnor won every math prize possible. Then there was Charles Fefferman, who got tenure at Princeton when he was 24! These people loomed large for me the way baseball stars or rock stars might loom for most other people. A part of me wondered what it was about them that let them see so much farther than I did. I spent an afternoon with André Weil, who revolutionized the field of algebraic geometry and when I asked him the secret to his success, he said "at an age younger than I was supposed to be I understood things I wasn't supposed to be able to understand." Translation: he didn't know any more than I did how he did it. The mystery was on both sides.

I went on to medical school and then to investing. I have spent most of my career running a biotech hedge fund. I bet on whether new products will succeed or fail in clinical trials or get FDA approval. I use many of the conceptual ideas I learned while studying mathematics to do my analysis. Many times this approach lets me make a very strong conclusion in advance of the data. In these cases, I can take a large bet and over the 13 years I have run the fund, I have had some real financial success. Still, a piece of me always wishes I had had the ability to be a great mathematician, the kind of mathematician included in this book. I think that there are many people like me and I hope that this book will inspire others to take another look at math and see it for its possibilities and excitement. We need to get beyond the stereotype that it is "hard" and only for a few special people.

There are many wonderful people who have been involved in the development of this book. Rather than thanking them individually, I send thanks to everyone collectively, knowing that you know who you are. Thanks!

LIST OF MATHEMATICIANS

Adebisi Agboola

Michael Artin

Michael Francis Atiyah

Manjul Bhargava

Bryan John Birch

Joan S. Birman

David Harold Blackwell

Enrico Bombieri

Richard Ewen Borcherds

Andrew Browder

Felix E. Browder

William Browder

Lennart Axel Edvard Carleson

Henri Cartan

Sun-Yung Alice Chang

Alain Connes

John Horton Conway

Kevin David Corlette

Ingrid Chantal Daubechies

Pierre Deligne

Persi Warren Diaconis

Simon Donaldson

Noam D. Elkies

Gerd Faltings

Charles Louis Fefferman

Robert Fefferman

Michael Freedman

Israel Moiseevich Gelfand

William Timothy Gowers

Phillip Griffiths

Mikhael Leonidovich Gromov

Benedict H. Gross

Robert Clifford Gunning

Eriko Hironaka

Heisuke Hironaka

Friedrich Hirzebruch

Vaughan Frederick Randal Jones

Nicholas Michael Katz

Robion Kirby

Frances Kirwan

Joseph John Kohn

János Kollár

Bertram Kostant

Harold William Kuhn

Robert Phelan Langlands

Peter David Lax

Robert D. MacPherson

Paul Malliavin

Benoit Mandelbrot

William Alfred Massey

John N. Mather

Barry Mazur

Dusa McDuff

Curtis McMullen

John Willard Milnor

Maryam Mirzakhani

Cathleen Synge Morawetz

David Mumford

John Forbes Nash, Jr.

Edward Nelson

Louis Nirenberg

George Olatokunbo Okikiolu

Kate Adebola Okikiolu

Andrei Okounkov

Roger Penrose

Arlie Petters

Marina Ratner

Kenneth Ribet

Peter Clive Sarnak

Marcus du Sautoy

Jean-Pierre Serre

James Harris Simons

Yakov Grigorevich Sinai

Isadore Manual Singer

Yum-Tong Siu

Stephen Smale

Elias Menachem Stein

Dennis Parnell Sullivan

Terence Chi-Shen Tao

Robert Endre Tarjan

John T. Tate

William Paul Thurston

Gang Tian

Burt Totaro

Karen Keskulla Uhlenbeck

Sathamangalam Rangaiyengar Srinivasa Varadhan

Michèle Vergne

Marie-France Vigneras

Avi Wigderson

Andrew John Wiles

Shing-Tung Yau

Don Zagier

ACKNOWLEDGMENTS

I am indebted to Brandon Fradd for suggesting I make these portraits of mathematicians and for supporting the project so generously. The enthusiasm of my editor at Princeton University Press, Vickie Kearn, has been remarkable and assured the book's integrity and elegance. Debbie Berne has been imaginative and a pleasure to work with in all phases of the book's design. Many thanks go to my assistant, Trellan Smith for her invaluable help and constant good cheer. And last but not least, much gratitude to my husband, Hans Kraus, and our daughter, Emily, for their encouragement and love.